6/02

BOA
EDITIONS
LIMITED

Books by W. D. Snodgrass

Poems

Heart's Needle
After Experience
Remains
The Führer Bunker: A Cycle of Poems in Progress
If Birds Build with Your Hair
The Boy Made of Meat
Magda Goebbels
Heinrich Himmler: Platoons and Files
D. D. Byrde Calling Jennie Wrenne
A Colored Poem (with DeLoss McGraw)
A Locked House
The Kinder Capers (with DeLoss McGraw)
Selected Poems 1957–1987
W. D.'s Midnight Carnival (with DeLoss McGraw)
The Midnight Carnival (with DeLoss McGraw)
To Shape a Song (with DeLoss McGraw)
The Death of Cock Robin (with DeLoss McGraw)
Autumn Variations
Snow Songs
Each in His Season
Spring Suite
The Fuehrer Bunker: The Complete Cycle

Essays

In Radical Pursuit

Translations

Gallows Songs, by Christian Morgenstern (with Lore Segal)
Six Troubadour Songs
Traditional Hungarian Songs
Six Minnesinger Songs
The Four Seasons
Star and Other Songs, by Mihai Eminescu

The Fuehrer Bunker

The Complete Cycle

Poems by
W. D. SNODGRASS

BOA EDITIONS, LTD.   ❋   BROCKPORT, NY   ❋   1995

LC #: 94–73437
ISBN: 1–880238–18–7 cloth
ISBN: 1–880238–19–5 paper

First Edition
95 96 97 98   7 6 5 4 3 2 1

The publication of books by BOA Editions, Ltd.,
is made possible with the assistance of grants from
the Literature Program of the New York State Council on the Arts
and the Literature Program of the National Endowment for the Arts,
as well as from the Lannan Foundation, the Lila Wallace–Reader's Digest
Literary Publishers Marketing Development Program,
the Rochester Area Foundation, the County of Monroe, NY, and contributions
by individual supporters.

Cover Design: Daphne Poulin
Typesetting: Richard Foerster
Manufacturing: McNaughton & Gunn, Lithographers
BOA Logo: Mirko

BOA Editions, Ltd.
A. Poulin, Jr., President
92 Park Avenue
Brockport, NY 14420

This book for
Kathleen

Contents

III
16 April 1945
THE RUSSIAN ATTACK

IV
20 April 1945
HITLER'S BIRTHDAY

V
22-23 April 1945
IDENTITIES

VI
24–27 April 1945
LOYALTIES

VII
28–30 April 1945
ORGY

VIII
1 May 1945
WAYS OUT

THE FUEHRER BUNKER

Even if we lose this war, we still win,
for our spirit will have penetrated our
enemies' hearts.
      — Joseph Goebbels

Mother Teresa, asked when it was she
started her work for abandoned children, replied,
"On the day I discovered I had a
Hitler inside me."

I

1 APRIL 1945
EASTER AND APRIL FOOLS' DAY

CHORUS: OLD LADY BARKEEP

*(During World War II, Berliners revived a
figure from Renaissance song and verse, Frau
Wirtin, for satirical verses, similar to limer-
icks and often obscene, about their leaders.)*

Old Lady Barkeep had a Folk
Who got their gun when Hitler spoke;
　　He bellowed, "Germany, waken!
Rise up; if any foe rejects us,
We'll broil their liver for our breakfast
　　And fry their balls like bacon!

"If they bite back, the bloody cunts,
We'll bang them on two fronts at once;
　　You can't resist a God!"
Like ladykillers at a dance,
His troops advanced in goosestep prance
Through Austria, Czechoslovakia, France,
　　Then found they'd shot their wad.

Easter in 1945
Was April Fools' Day. The one drive
They could maintain was to survive.
　　Through caves and cellar holes,
Ditches and subway tunnels then
These irresistible Supermen
　　Crept like ants or moles.

*　　*　　*

In Old Lady Barkeep's shrunken Reich
Herr Dr. Goebbels took the mike
　　And vowed in his grand style:
"If it costs all your lives, my dears,
Our reign will last a thousand years!
　　Or twelve — same price. Sieg: HEIL!"

15

DR. JOSEPH GOEBBELS
MINISTER FOR PROPAGANDA

—1 April 1945, 0930 hours.

*(At a French window of his villa on the
Wannsee, he watches a 1000-plane air raid
over Berlin. He sings a folk song from the re-
ligious wars of the 1600's.)*

Days, American bombing flights
Crush us to ash and brick dust; nights,
The British burn us down. Up there,
None of our own planes anywhere.
Revive, rise, you Powers of the Air —
It's Easter! Ha! — we haven't got a prayer!

Pray, children, pray;
Swedes are on their way.

So "Red Berlin" burns — turning red
Again. Those same streets piled with dead
Where we once cracked men's skulls to win
Their hearts and high offices. Once in,
We swore we'd never leave except
Feet first — one promise we *have* kept.
Maybe we should have warned them, though:
Let this earth tremble when we go!

Oxenstiern will march this way
Teaching children how to pray.

[turns from window]

First time I saw a bombed-out city —
Dresden — corrupted me with pity.
Some suffocated, others burned

Alive; for lack of air, some turned
Black and hard — their body fat ran
Out like goose grease in a pan.

Then he'll roast the fat, young pullets;
Melt church windows down for bullets.

I clumped down those long stacks of dead
Weeping, weeping. Back here, I said
I wanted the full power for putting
This whole nation on a war footing.
Now the foe's halfway through our gate
The Chief gives me the power. Too late.

Bet, kinder, bet.

So once more, the Chief's wrong proves out
Better than my right. I, no doubt,
Could have curbed slaughter, ruin, terror —
Just my old sentimental error.
Our role is to wipe out a twisted
Life that should never have existed.

Morgen komm der Schwed:

Each Ami bomb, each Russian shell
Helps us to wipe away this hell
Called Europe, Man's age-old, unjust
Network of lies, pandering, lust,
Deformity. This is to be
Young again — idealistic, free.

Morgen komm der Oxenstjerna

Once, my newscasters would disguise
Each loss as a triumph. Those lies
Were mere truths *we* misunderstood:
There's no evil we can't find good.

Will der kinder beten lerne.

[turns back to the window]

Let it all fall in, burn and burst.
Blest be who dares act out his worst
Impulses, give way to the thirst
For blood and show this for the accursed
Inferno we took it for, right from the first.

Bet, kinder, bet;
Pray, children, pray.

Our Father who art in Nihil,
We thank Thee for this day of trial
And for the loss that teaches self-denial.
Amen.

Old Lady Barkeep had a Bormann;
He'd been an agricultural foreman
    Then spent a year in prison —
He'd killed a Red. Still, that's the norm and
Nowadays he's Hitler's doorman.
    How are the lowly risen!

The Fuehrer's watchdog secretary
Blocked every rival who could carry
    News of loss or disaster.
    While fresh defeats came faster, vaster,
He screened our Leader's mail or phonecalls,
Turning him deaf and blind as stone walls;
    Now guess who's the Master?

*   *   *

Bormann's poor wife got a bewilderin'
Headful of doctrines, houseful of children
    While he strove like a demon
Seducing other girls non-stop
But sent home love-notes full of slop
    Like towels smeared with semen.

MARTIN BORMANN
PERSONAL SECRETARY TO THE FUEHRER

— 1 April 1945, 0930 hours.

*(At his desk, he writes his wife while calcu-
lating his status in the Nazi hierarchy.)*

The Fuehrer Bunker, Berlin.
Easter!

Dearest Beloved Momsy Girl,

Our hour of Destiny is born! The Reds have scraped up every last Slav
lout to hurl at us. Every day more tanks, troops, armor.

> I win; win; win. Not one phone call,
> One letter gets past to the Chief.
> My enemies drop off like leeches.

Upstairs, 1,000 American planes are bombing us this minute. Our
Luftwaffe, of course, is nowhere to be seen.

> So fat Goering don't dare show his face.
> Out at his estate with all his womenfolk,
> Fine wines, all that luxury.

Oh Momsy, such times I miss you most. Send 50 pounds at least of
honey to the shelter. I'll see to dried vegetables myself.

> No way he could succeed the Chief now.
> If I could just get the proof he's back
> On drugs. This time, paracodeine.

Our dear old "Onkle Heinrich" — Himmler himself — has lost his
command at Army Group Vistula.

Knew it; knew he'd fuck himself when I
Got him that post. And that butthead
Thanked me "for my kind help!"

We mustn't never forsake them in their trials. Still got his SS troops,
concentration camps, Gestapo.

Still my worst enemy. Still got
All Europe shitting pink. Good reason:
Ten million Jews and Slavs.

Do they plan to get captured by the Americans? Himmler could get
shot for...no....Why not take his wife some of your homemade jam?

Some kind of proof he was in on the July
Bombplot on the Chief. And he must have peace
Feelers to the West; that's treason!

Himmler's post has gone to Heinrici — regular Army man. And Speer
just got back all his offices.

Heinrici never even joined the party. We'll
Keep an eye on Speer. Goebbels is no threat.
He means it: he'll kill himself.

In such times, our Leader needs real heroes. Like you and me, sweet
Momsy, true Nazis that think only how to save our people.

Got them by the gonads, every one of them.
Another heavy blast! Thank the Lord we're
Under 12 feet of solid concrete.

Us, with our innate love of light — forced by the Jews to live like
creatures of the underworld — that just fills me with rage!

Thine alone,

Martin

Old Lady Barkeep's Himmler, tiny,
For 10 long years plunked his Reichsheinie
    On a piano stool.
No music came of this. The fact is,
His teacher said, "If you won't practice,
    I'll pay *you,* you fool!"

*   *   *

Old Lady Barkeep's SS leader,
Himmler, failed as a chicken breeder.
    Though flustery as a hen,
    He made the world his pen
Where he played cock for the human flock
    And hatched out Supermen.

*   *   *

Old Lady Barkeep had a Himmler;
He thought leading the SS similar
    To being Christ or Pope;
His mission held one small perversion:
He strove for all mankind's conversion
    To little bars of soap.
He trusted star charts and the occult;
In hard times, what else to consult
    For one small ray of hope?

```
HEINRICH · HIMMLER
REICHSFUEHRER · SS
FORMER · COMMANDER
ARMY · GROUP · VISTULA

· 1 · APRIL · 1945 · 1100 · HOURS ·
```

(Stripped of command, Himmler withdraws to his sanatorium at Hohenlychen where he tries to cast his horoscope. MM = 76.)

```
A S T R A L · S I G N S · S U G G E S T · W E · M I G H T ·
B E · I N · T R O U B L E · D U R I N G · A P R I L · B U T
C O N C U R · O U R · L U C K · W I L L · T U R N · A L L ·
D A N G E R · W I L L · B E · A V E R T E D · A T · T H E ·
E L E V E N T H · H O U R · W E · W I L L · B E · S A V E D

F O R T U N A T E L Y · B Y · A · S U D D E N · D E A T H ·
G O O D · G R I E F · I · D O · H O P E · B U T · I S · I T
H I T L E R S · D E A T H · T H E · S U N · I N   L I B R A
I N D I C A T E S · T H E · F A L L · O F · P R I N C E S ·
J U P I T E R · U R A N U S · I N · S A G I T T A R I U S ·

K E E P S · P R O M I S I N G · A · B R E A K T H R O U G H
L A R G E · O P P O R T U N I T I E S · F O R · G R O W T H
M A N Y · N E W · C H A N C E S · F O R · C E L E B R I T Y
N A T U R A L · T I M I D I T Y · C H A N G I N G · I N T O
O P E N · B O L D N E S S · N A T U R A L · T I M I D I T Y

P E R H A P S · T H E Y · D I D N T · R E A L L Y · M E A N
Q U I T E · T H A T · M E A N T I M E · M Y · S I G N · O F
R O Y A L · C H A N C E · P R O V E S · I · A M · T O · B E
S U C C E S S O R · T O · T H E · C H I E F · F U R T H E R
T H I S · S I G N · I S · W E L L · A S P E C T E D · B Y ·

U R A N U S · C O N J U N C T · J U P I T E R · W E · M A Y
V E R Y · W E L L · L O S E · T H E   W A R · B U T · I L L
W I N · A S S U M E · P O W E R · A F T E R · A L L · I F ·
Y O U · C A N T · P U T · Y O U R · F A I T H · I N · T H E
Z O D I A C · J U S T · W H A T · C A N · Y O U · T R U S T
```

CHORUS: OLD LADY BARKEEP

Old Lady Barkeep's tough old General
Heinrici said, "Our seasoned men are all
   Stalwart despite defeats.
We fought for lightning victories once —
Then we had trucks, planes, tanks and guns —
   Now it's for *slow* retreats."

COL. GEN. GOTTHARD HEINRICI
COMMANDER, ARMY GROUP VISTULA

—1 April 1945.

(Replacing Himmler, Heinrici faced the Russians in the North and East. At his HQ at Prenzlau, he leaves the Easter morning service.)

Army Group Vistula? Ghosts! The ghost
Of ghosts! A name they dreamed up
With the Vistula already lost. Now,
Fifty five miles from Berlin, we have
New orders: stand fast on the Oder with
Names, mere names of once great armies:
Manteuffel's Third Panzers; the Ninth.
Their trained men, supplies, chains of command
Gone. Dead. Ghosts. To redeem
Us of our faults. The High Command
Assures me those two and one half million
Russians on the far bank are not there.
Twenty thousand guns. Six thousand tanks.
Not there. Ghosts too, no doubt. And
This preacher dares say to our faces
That we shall rise up from these ruins,
This grave, and be born again. We may
Be God's sons; *some* of the dead
Stay dead. How many of the living can
Match that and just stay alive — how many?

```
HEINRICH • HIMMLER
REICHSFUEHRER • SS
FORMER • COMMANDER
ARMY • GROUP • VISTULA

• 1 • APRIL • 1945 • 1105 • HOURS •
```

(Himmler continues. Field Marshal Keitel and
General Jodl were joint heads of the German
High Command and Hitler's toadies.)

```
AND • I • DO • DESERVE • IT • TRUE • THESE
BUNGLING • GENERALS • DID • GET • THIS
COMMAND • FOULED • UP • WHAT • COULD • I
DO • COMING • SO • LATE • IN • THE • GAME •
EVEN • SO • HE • BLAMES • ME • FOR • THEIR

FAILURES • I • MUST • GET • ON • MY • FEET
GET • BACK • TO • BERLIN • AS • FOR • THIS
HEINRICI • HES • NO • FLAMING • GENIUS
I • DONT • SEE • HIM • WINNING • BATTLES
JODL • & • KEITEL • PLEASE • NOTE • THEY

KEEP • TELLING • THE • CHIEF • HORRID •
LIES • ABOUT • ME • AND • SO • DO • SPEER •
MARTIN • BORMANN • GOEBBELS • THERES
NO • ONE • BUT • FEGELEIN • TO • PUT • IN •
ONE • GOOD • WORD • FOR • ME • EVERYONE •

POISONS • HIM • AGAINST • ME • ON • THE •
Q • T • BUT • JUST • YOU • WAIT • TIL • THIS
RUSSIAN • ATTACK • ON • BERLIN • GETS •
STARTED • HEINRICI • WONT • LOOK • SO •
TALENTED • YET • EVEN • THAT • MAY • GET

UGLY • TOO • IF • BERLIN • FALLS • O • THE
VERITABLE • MARTYRDOM • I • UNDERGO •
WHY • MY • CRAMPS • ARE • COMING • BACK •
YOU • KNOW • IM • NOT • FIT • FOR • COMBAT
ZONES • IM • GOING • BACK • & • LIE • DOWN
```

CHORUS: OLD LADY BARKEEP

Old Lady Barkeep had a Goering;
He bragged, in everybody's hearing,
    "I swear, as a great flyer,
If just one German city's bombed,
    You can call me 'Meier.'"
Now every puny town's on fire;
Rubble's piled up higher and higher;
Come dance around the funeral pyre;
    Sing: Meier! Meier! Meier!

REICHSMARSCHALL HERMANN GOERING

— 1 April 1945.

*(Goering, a World War I ace, now head of the
Luftwaffe, is in deep disgrace for its failures.
At his Karinhall estate, he quizzes himself.)*

And why, Herr Reichsmarschall, is Italy
Just like schnitzle? *If they're beaten,*
Either one of them gets bigger.
Neither cuts too firm a figure.
Still, all this humble pie you've eaten
Lately stuffs YOU out quite prettily.

So then, Herr Goering, how can we
Tell you and Italy apart?
Italy always wins by losing;
Meanwhile I, adroitely using
High skills and cunning, mastered the art
Of flat disgrace through victory.

You led our Flying Circus; how
Could our war ace become a clown?
Both pad out extended fronts;
Both make their living from slick stunts;
All the same, both get shot down.
But only one's called Meier now.

Pray, could an old, soft football be
Much like a man in deep disgrace?
They don't kick back; don't even dare
Look up — the British own the air!
So, stick a needle in someplace;
Pump yourself full of vacancy.

But answer one more question, which is:
Are politicians like whipped cream?
Both will inflate themselves with gas;
Also, they both puff up your ass
Till you're exposed like some bad dream
Where you've grown too big for your britches.

Herr President, can we tell apart
An artful statesman from an ass?
Fat chance! One spouts out high ideals;
One makes low rumblings after meals.
But that's the threat of leaking gas
That all men fear! *Right — that's a fart.*

Last, could you give one simple rule
To tell a medal from a turd?
Both of them come from those above you
Delivering their true opinion of you.
Right! Here's your new medal, conferred
For vast achievements: April Fool!

CHORUS: OLD LADY BARKEEP

Old Lady Barkeep's architect
Was hired by Hitler to erect
    Cities and monuments
But then got named to be his minister
For armaments, a somewhat sinister
    Refinement of events.

*   *   *

Old Lady Barkeep's builder, Speer,
Created citadels in air,
    Cathedrals made of ice.
Massed aerial searchlights formed this clever
Illusion in the skies but never
    Brought light to their price.

ALBERT SPEER
ARMAMENTS MINISTER

— 1 April 1945, 2230 hours.

*(Hitler's architect and friend, Speer had ear-
lier been dismissed for admitting the war was
lost. Reinstated on 31 March, he emerges from
the Bunker steps.)*

So
I am
Reborn?
For Easter?
Hitler's builder
Once more. But not to
Build. To turn out armor,
Supplies for a war we cannot win,
Equipment to tear down this world, not
Build another. We sit together, he and I,
Like little boys playing with toy train models
Of his new Linz and Munich, of his vast, new Berlin.

And is it wise, getting back in his good graces when
he is failing, when our enemies are closing in
on all sides, when his power will soon be
gone? Easier to accuse me as one of
those who helped him burn down
their cities, who killed
their young men to
build cloud
castles,
toys.

Every
Day the
Originals
Crash down. He
Swears to me he will
Not defend Berlin, which
Would mean to destroy Berlin.
I swear I still have faith, which
Means I'll destroy anything he orders.
Then I tell his generals, gauleiters, our
Factory managers to ignore his direct command
For total destruction, a charred, barren land. Lord,
Lord, who ever said you can't build on lies?

CHORUS: OLD LADY BARKEEP

Old Lady Barkeep found a mistress
To comfort Hitler in his distress
    When all plans went to ruin.
But for prestigious, high style wooin',
Disclosure to the public's viewin',
Even old-fashioned bill and cooin',
    Or just plain screwin,
    Nothin' doin'.

EVA BRAUN

—1 April 1945.

*(At her apartment in the Reich Chancellery,
Hitler's mistress imagines showing her snap-
shot album to a visitor sometime after her
own death. She sings American popular
songs.)*

You've heard of Eva Braun, of course — His lover?
Here's one of EVA AT NINETEEN — something
That Heinrich Hoffmann, His own photographer
Took just for Him. *This half-cooked dumpling?*
When you could have beauty queens, why take her?

Oh, believe it, beloved, because it's true,

Maybe He felt that, in a time of trial,
If every other force, if his own nation
Failed Him, with lies, cowardice and betrayal
On all sides, that these two — here, His Alsatian
Bitch named BLONDI — these two would stay loyal.

You're all that I want you to be.

HER BEDROOM AT THE BERGHOF — His connected.
He passed her off as a mere housekeeper, though?
Stenographer. Such things were just expected
Inside the circle. *And outside? Who would know*
Such a person so much as existed?

I'm telling everyone I know
That I'm the one who loves you so.

GRETL'S WEDDING — You know that Eva's little
Sister married an SS General — Fegelein?
The Chief Himself brought that about. *Yet Hitler*
Refused to marry Eva? She was resigned

To that. *And to leave having kids to Gretl?*

Tell me it's not true...

GYMNASTICS — you can see she had a lively
time of it. Here we have GAMES IN THE SNOW;
here's EVA AS MAY QUEEN, EVA DIVING
AT LAKE GARDA. *He's never with her, though.*
Here: STROLLING — right together, side by side.

Anything I do...

LUNCHEON AT THE TEAHOUSE: always afterwards
they'd sit together like this — holding hands
like an old married couple. *He's dozed off — bored
I'd guess.* There were such terrible demands,
He'd be worn out, tired...He just worked so hard.

**Everyone says you're turning from me
For a love that's new.**

SUNBATHING IN THE NUDE — but then of course
we can't show that. *We've heard about a hush-hush
film she had made of certain acts he forced
her to perform. Then, if he tried to flush
her someday....* We know nothing of that sort.

**Tell me that you love me just the same;
That's all I want from you.**

Can films lie? Not these. She saved
these candid snapshots as a true
image, brought back to life, preserved,
of a joyful life that no one knew,
of a great love no one believed.

**I can't believe
That you believe in me.**

Old Lady Barkeep had a Hitler
Who seemed an average man or littler,
Then climbed out on a high branch, brittler
    Than any circus wire.
He said, "Up here, no man's my equal,
So I can perch calm as an eagle
    Above life's muck and mire."

But like all those that find their berth,
Mortal, on this muddy earth,
    He soon made a profound
Discovery what his life was worth:
    One hole, deep in the ground.
Still if enough men, for his sake,
Passed into cold clay first, he'd make
    His name live on, renowned.

ADOLF HITLER

— 1 April 1945, 2330 hours.

*(In the bunker's deepest level, Hitler sits be-
fore the wall map in his conference room.)*

Down: I got it all. Almost.

[takes situation reports]

Traitors! Heidelberg and Danzig handed over
Practically undamaged. Some half a million
Squirm out of our glory.

Brat fed sick on sugartits.

And Magdeburg? Bremen? Who could we send
To make their lives worth less to them?

Say that I spoiled my appetite.

Our best troops, sacked up in the Ruhr —
Too gutless even to get killed.

"Casualties? But that is what
The young men are there for."

In our camps,
You tramp them down in ditches like dead leaves;
Nights, they squirm up through the offal....

Always this soft side mounting up,

Speer would let these ditchworms spawn....
And yesterday I put Speer back in office.
Truly, you regret how kind you've been.

My mother's cake-and-candy boy.

[throws down a report]

Americans at their Easter mass. Sick,
Snivelling, Jew Jesus of these Christians!

        Always my own worst enemy. Let them,
        My own half-brother, Alois, let them

...my brother-in-arms, Ernst Roehm, who
stood against me, slip away. Then dared
come back. On every side, my mercies
gathering against me.

        With my mother, my own way. She
        Rammed it down the old man's throat.
        Her open grave's mouth, speaking:
        Did I choose I should die?

Then, then, we hacked them down like trash rats.
All who'd learned too little. Or too much.
In sewers, ditches, let them lay. Let them be seen.

        And this ground would devour me.
        So shall I swallow all this ground
        Till we two shall be one flesh.

Before my firing squads, men heiled my name.
The Old Man, Hindenburg, praised my
Swift gallantry. From ten million speakers
My voice scattering like the farmers' rain.

        The evils I do not desire,
        I do and I survive.

My nerves rang one, one with the iron worlds;
I moved among the Old Powers, past
Evil, past time or consequence once more.

What crime I choose is
God's Law; my lie, truth.
Too late. The Powers move on.

[takes up the reports]

Too late. Crude populations rising.

This left arm shaking, pinned down
By the right.

Deserters. Traitors.

Since Stalingrad fell,
This shuddering I can't control.

April. In our bombed-out gardens pale leaf buds,
That sickly green scum, filming the trees again.
Through cracked concrete green shoots shove up to the light.

[at his desk, writes an order]

Well, we can still provide an Easter Fools' gift,
Give them something to look up to: a wartime decoration —
More deserters to hang up on their streetlamps.
Stalin: count on his appetite. The leavings — belts, bones,
Buckles — nothing sticks in *that* man's craw.

So; we must go out now. Suppose
We could still find a little chocolate cake?
A teensy bit of schlag, perhaps?

II

5 – 15 APRIL 1945
PREPARATIONS

CHORUS: OLD LADY BARKEEP

Old Lady Barkeep had a Reich
Where people looked and thought alike
Since Slav and Gypsy, queer and kike
  Got killed — wasn't that purer?
"We'll scrub their bloodstains off our wall
Then we'll grow into handsome, tall,
Blonde, blue-eyed Aryans one and all —
  Like Goebbels or our Fuehrer!"

    * * *

Old Lady Barkeep had a Fuehrer
Who said he'd make his Folk securer
And all their future bloodlines surer:
  He'd just let some bad blood.
Still, do dark hair and eyes denote him
The man to be all Aryans' totem?
With only one ball in your scrotum,
  How can you stand at stud?

COL. GEN. GOTTHARD HEINRICI
COMMANDER, ARMY GROUP VISTULA

—8 April 1945.

*(The Allies advance on all fronts. At the daily
Bunker conference, Heinrici had urged Hitler
to strengthen Berlin's forces.)*

Worse than, less than ghosts. Bodies.
When I got here, a shakedown; an SS body search!
How far we've come! Fifteen feet down,
Underneath the city's sewers, the Fuehrer
In dark glasses (don't they call those
Blinders?) sneering, "Berlin? A mere
Diversion. The real attack will be...."
Same thing he'd said to call us back
From Moscow. How far we've come since then!
Still, I had convinced him: save Biehler's men
From Frankfurt, eighteen battalions —
Commit them here, now. Goering, then:
The grand gesture: "My Fuehrer, I offer you
100,000 Airmen." So then
Raeder: "20,000 Seamen." Next
ReichsHeinie: "15,000 SS men."
He rescinds his order; Biehler's men
Go back to die for nothing. While we
Defend Berlin with what? With bodies. We could
Quite as well send children, children's pets,
Old men in wheelchairs, against the tanks.
Thank God nobody offered any! So far
Down, the toilets must flush up! Thank God
They can't frisk down a man's thoughts!
A body search! Someone might smuggle in
One live brain cell. Nothing but bodies here,
Not quite corpses just yet — just bodies.

```
HEINRICH•HIMMLER
REICHSFUEHRER•SS
FORMER•COMMANDER
ARMY•GROUP•VISTULA

•9•APRIL•1945•
```

*(As major cities and defense points fall, con-
centration camps are threatened, especially
Bergen-Belsen and Buchenwald. MM=74.)*

```
ANY•TRULY•MODERN•STUDY•OF•THE•
BRAIN•MUST•COOLLY•METHODICALLY
CONSIDER•THE•RACES•PROGRESS•&•
DEVELOPMENT•WE•MUST•MAKE•EVERY
EFFORT•TO•ISOLATE•THE•CRUCIAL•

FACTORS•THAT•MAKE•SOME•PEOPLES
GREAT•WHILE•OTHERS•DEGENERATE•
HUMANITY•CANNOT•AFFORD•TO•WAIT
IVE•HAD•MY•MEN•GATHER•1000S•OF
JEWISH•SKULLS•WE•MEASURE•WEIGH

KEEP•COMPLETE•RECORDS•&•BEFORE
LONG•COULD•NO•DOUBT•SOLVE•THIS
MYSTERY•ABOVE•ALL•ELSE•DEVOTED
NAZIS•MUST•KEEP•A•SCIENTIFIC•&
OBJECTIVE•VIEW•IF•WE•WANT•REAL

PROGRESS•IVE•INVESTIGATED•THIS
QUITE•THOROUGHLY•OUR•DARK•AGE•
RECORDS•SHOW•1000S•WENT•TO•THE
STAKE•PEOPLE•HONESTLY•BELIEVED
THEM•TO•BE•WITCHES•ITS•SIMPLY•

UNTHINKABLE•MONSTROUS•WASTING•
VALUABLE•GERMAN•BLOOD•TO•BURN•
WITCHES•THAT•JUST•GOES•TO•SHOW
YOU•WHAT•FOLLY•&•INSANE•EXCESS
ZEALOTS•&•FANATICS•CAN•FALL•TO

ALL•OUR•WORK•THO•IS•ENDANGERED
BY•THIS•BARBAROUS•ONSLAUGHT•OF
COMMUNISTIC•HORDES•SINCE•SUCH•
DULL•HALF-CIVILIZED•BRUTES•ARE
ENEMIES•TO•TRUE•CULTURE•&•THE•
```

FULLY • ANALYTICAL • MIND • WE • MUST •
GATHER • ALL • RECORDS • AND • REMAINS
HIDE • ANY • EVIDENCE • WHICH • COULD •
INDICATE • WHAT • WEVE • DONE • THATS •
JUST • AS • VITAL • NOW • AS • IT • IS • TO •

KEEP • ALL • THE • CAMPS • CLEANED • OUT
LABORATORIES • MUST • BE • TORN • DOWN
MOVED • OR • THOROUGHLY • DISGUISED •
NEW • TITLES • SHOULD • BE • ISSUED • TO
OUR • DOCTORS • AND • TECHNICIANS • I •

PALE • TO • THINK • WHAT • SOME • MIGHT •
QUITE • POSSIBLY • IMAGINE • IF • THEY
ROOTED • INTO • THE • MASS • GRAVES • OR
SOME • OF • OUR • BOLDER • EXPERIMENTS
THEYD • MISUNDERSTAND • IT • CALL • US

UNPRINCIPLED • HOODLUMS • GIVEN • TO
VICIOUS • INSTINCTS • THEYD • CLAIM •
WE • HAD • LOST • ALL • CONSCIENCE • AND
YIELDED • TO • THE • WORSHIP • OF • BAAL
ZOROASTER • SOMETHING • BARBAROUS •

ALBERT SPEER
ARMAMENTS MINISTER

—12 April 1945.

(Near Prenzlau on the Eastern front, Speer has just met with Heinrici and Gen. Reymann, Commandant of Berlin, to subvert Hitler's "scorched earth" directive.)

We
Saved
The bridges
Into Berlin today;
Two million people will
Have gas, coal, power, water,
Food; have some chance to survive.
General Reymann has orders, Heinrici's
And mine, to blow up only bridges with no
Gas mains, water pipes, electric cables. We have
Broken our oaths, defied our Fuehrer's direct orders.
We tear down the order of our lives, hoping to save lives.

What can his order to destroy these bridges mean, but that
he will defend Berlin, after promising to let it live?
So I obey his promise, but not his direct command.
I have saved these bridges, at the risk of
my own life — saved them not from the
Russians, but *for* the Russians.
Will they spare any more of
us than Hitler would?
Will they spare me
for opening our
gates to
them?

Yet
We have
Saved these
Lives; that cannot
Be otherwise than good.
Have saved these Germans, not
From the Russian guns, but saved
Them from their own leaders. To whom
They stay loyal. They would have me hanged
For disobeying him even though it saved their lives.
Surely the West must move in to save the city. Patton
Is in position to attack; is he one to obey insane orders?

Whoever takes this city, somebody must run things; and all
    the rest are unfit or incompetent. Every one of them,
        Goebbels, Goering, Himmler, certain of the noose.
            I have shown I can build, can rebuild; shown
                I can save what's needed. So do I think
                    I've saved my own position, my own
                        neck? Think I have built my
                            own way out? No, these
                                bridges won't save
                                    me, not even
                                        in my own
                                            eyes.

REICHSMARSCHALL HERMANN GOERING

— 13 April 1945.

*(The Luftwaffe's new Me262's, the world's
first jet fighters, have been decimated over
Berlin because altered by Hitler to serve as
bombers. Goering imagines himself inter-
viewed by figures he takes for accountants.)*

Sir, sir, we must check your accounts,
Fill out the nation's last reports.
The Reds might ask if our books balance.
*What fool keeps books? I've used my talents
At hunting, hawking, the noble sports
Of counts....* And certain no-accounts?

My friends are my own business. Mine.
One of your businesses. Of course
You HAVE the Hermann Goering Works....?
*Damned right I do — and not one man shirks
His duty on my labor force.
There's not one thing there out of line.*

Then could you list your stock on hand,
Physical plants, materiel,
Capital and other assets?
*In a pig's ass. While my own ass sets
Squat on the throne, no ledgers tell
How far and wide I might expand.*

Your tools, then? *Tools? Hah! Men of bad
Conscience. They do just what they're told
Or else you hang the sons of bitches.*
Still, rumors abound of your great riches;
What could become of those tenfold
Means and resources you once had?

49

I had nerve and drive, the abilities
That lead men in the paths of glory;
I'm still called Iron Man, the Stout German.
Let's just say we can't determine,
Right now, your complete inventory.
At this rate, who needs liabilities?

Still you must have some? *Some?* Some. *Friends.*
Those no-accounts I counted on.
Then they gave you the works! Tisk, tisk!
You can't fire friends. I took the risk
And kept them on. Once the iron was gone...?
And their pet projects reached bad ends...?

We come, then, to bad debts. You owe...
To Adolf Hitler, loyalty.
Then it's no great loss...you've no qualms
He took your new jets to haul bombs?
Not save your cities? *That may be;*
You can't brand me his yes man. No?

You told him, then, that this was nonsense?
I did not; I've not lost my mind.
Still, as a man who's kept his nerve...
My oath, my duty is to serve
Our Leader and to render blind
Obedience.... Yes; "men of bad conscience...."

Sir — now you'll forgive me — but I'm
Certain these records have been tampered with!
Friend, that had better be a joke.
The Reds are closing in; our folk
Must have a positive, unsullied myth.
We can't have quibbling all the time.

Of course not. We don't mean to sound
Unsympathetic to the New Man.
We realize statesmen must be able
To work things out under the table.
Men have their price; your acts were human.
Still, you could just spread some around...?

FIELD MARSHAL ERNST BUSCH
COMMANDER-IN-CHIEF, NORTH WEST

—14 April 1945, 1000 hours.

*(Busch, fresh from his front lines against the
British, his uniform dishevelled, waits in the
hallway to see Hitler. He has been talking to
Traudl Junge, a young secretary.)*

"That Bohemian corporal," growled Hindenburgh.
Just. Just. And he has mastered
Us. Overmastered us. Outfaced us.
Victory in our reach, he called us back
From Moscow. Let the British troops escape
From Dunkirk. Our own men, though, could not escape
From Stalingrad. Hurls us into a two-front war
Then interferes in every minute
Detail of operations past his grasp. On the level
Of a corporal. Abandoned
To the whims of that wastrel, Goering;
To that stammering idiot
Himmler. With his death squads
Cancering the East. Vienna
Fallen today. And we
Can't last two weeks. Any man of honor
Would have made peace six months ago
Then shot himself. A gentleman, an officer
In any lost cause knows his duty is to report
Precisely that situation. I have told
This secretary my irreversible intention....

TRAUDL JUNGE

—14 April 1945, 1010 hours.

*(The youngest of Hitler's secretaries, Traudl
Humps, married Hitler's SS valet, Hans Junge.
To form his own view of the war, he requested
active duty; he was killed in action.)*

they know but never tell me
what they know   back from the fighting
what made my good hans
alien   lost from all our ways
lost from each other   that our Chief
just did not know   had no idea
my mother when their house
got burned down   if that Hitler
of yours had the least   at least
someone will let Him know now
back from the fighting   who has seen
the young men like my good hans
beautiful   open hearted   dying

FIELD MARSHAL ERNST BUSCH
COMMANDER-IN-CHIEF, NORTH WEST

—14 April 1945, 1035 hours.

(Busch emerges from his talk with Hitler, refreshed but embarrassed.)

What could I have had in mind? To have
Forgotten his successes — how he led us on
Into the Saar, the Rhineland, into Austria,
Czechoslovakia, Poland, France, while we
Held back and said it was all impossible?
Who saved us, standing firm that first winter
When we would have retreated in a rout?
Whose iron determination, and whose...
And those eyes, the eyes! We must forget....
And let us hope that that young woman will
Forget this unfortunate aberration, this lapse
Of faith, this flight from true reality.
A momentary madness. And, of course,
The secret weapons he's held back until
The auspicious moment. But, obviously,
The word of an officer, a gentleman, a
Field Marshal, will always be accepted
Against a secretary's....

DR. JOSEPH GOEBBELS
MINISTER FOR PROPAGANDA

—15 April 1945.

*(Imaginary headlines run through Goebbels'
mind with quotes from Carlyle and Goethe.)*

Two days ago, we heard about
Roosevelt's death. I'd driven out
To the Eastern front where our men wait
For this Red drive to seal their fate.
I told them how, once, Frederick the Great
Despaired, lost all hope,

*Wait yet a little while, brave king,
for the sun of your good fortune....*

                  then the death
Of the Czarina Elizabeth
Saved him; once more, some miracle
Must save us. They were skeptical
At best — while I believed it least of all.

We drove back here to find Berlin
A trash dump — buildings crumpling in,
Streets full of smoking masonry.
Then, when we reached the Ministry,
Semmler came bustling out and said,
"Sir! Great news! Roosevelt is dead!"

GREAT WAR CRIMINAL
PAYS FOR HIS CRIMES

Blinded by hope, I took that bait:
"Break out the best champagne! Our Fate
Smiles!" — called in editors, reporters,
Phoned the Chief, phoned our headquarters

At the Eastern front so I could crow
"Who's right now? Didn't I tell you so?"

GERMAN FORCES
TRIUMPH ONCE MORE

Two days have passed; I can attest
At least our champagne *was* the best.

Just one thing always kept my eyes
Fox-bright to outwit or surprise
My foes: I knew which of my lies *were* lies.
Some of these stuffed shirts still believe
We have "miracle weapons" up our sleeve.
Today, one lame brain dared suggest
We might separate East from West
Through "friendly overtures to the Pope!"

> *If a will-o'-the-wisp has guided thee,*
> *Don't ask for too much certainty.*

High time I learned to give up hope
That Fate puts out, bends to men's wishes
Or spread her legs for our ambitious
Hankerings. What she puts out is grief,
While I play pimp, selling belief
To fools. I must go sell some to the Chief.

MAGDA GOEBBELS

—15 April 1945.

*(Goebbels' sister has offered to take the
Goebbels' six children to evade the Russians.)*

Now Joseph's sister's offered us the chance
    To send the children somewhere farther West
Into the path of the Americans
    To let them live. It might be for the best

To send the children somewhere; farther West —
    They could surrender there. It stands to reason
To let them live; it might be for the best,
    Yet our Fuehrer would brand that as flat treason.

They could surrender. There: it stands to reason
    You ought to save the few souls dear to you,
Yet our Fuehrer would brand that as flat treason
    To all we've thought. To be upright and true,

You ought to save the few souls dear to you,
    Though their survival could no doubt bring shame
To all we've thought to be upright and true.
    Living with strangers, they'd still bear our name,

Though their survival could no doubt bring shame,
    The way they'd live. They'd have to turn — once there,
Living with strangers. They'd still bear our name
    With our past that could be too much to bear.

The way they'd live, they'd have to turn, once there,
    Into the path of the Americans
With our past. *That* could be too much to bear,
    Now Joseph's sister's offered us the chance.

EVA BRAUN

—15 April 1945.

*(Air raids have forced Eva to move to the
Bunker. Her arrival struck dread in those
already there. Raised a Catholic, she recalls
parts of the Requiem Mass.)*

There they go, behind my back, whispering
About me. Somebody said I would be
"Death's Angel." So I bring them news
They all already know: that they will die.

> *Dies illa, dies irae*
> *calamitatis et miseriae,*

Seems that I'm getting up in their world,
Their life down this badger hole, this
Cement submarine. Promoted in the field. Once
It was the Merry Widow, the Dumb Cow.
I christened myself Miss No-Private-Life.

> *quando caeli movendi et terra:*

The bombers, thousands, thousands, they have
Wings sure enough, they carry our bad news.
They drove me, just the same as they
Drove them, down here. The smoke, the stench,
Sirens, walls collapsing. Just the same
As them, I will die here. But by his side.

> *Tremens factus sum ego, et timeo,*

We will all die here just the same as we
Would up there. Almost as soon. Only I,
I assign myself here. We know we will die.
I assign myself how, where, who with.

de veneris judicare
saeculum per ignem.

Now all their muttering is suicide: a pistol
In the mouth, cyanide. I will pick poison.
My body must go unmarked, must be found
Beautiful, found worthy to have lived,
Worthy to be found here next to Him.

dies magna et amara valde.

Death's Angel should be better dressed.
This tailored gray suit will never do.
Grandmother's black silk stayed in Munich.
This topaz pendant, my silver fox coat, my black
Lace underthings to show how He adorned me.

dona eis, Domine,

And let them find my big bed, crammed
In down here, my massive dresser, crested
With the initials, E.B., of my name, worked
In the design of my own lucky four-leaf clovers.

Requiem aeternam.

LT. GEN. HELMUTH "BONY KARL" WEIDLING
COMMANDER, 56th PANZER CORPS

—15 April 1945.

*(At his improvised HQ on the Eastern front,
Weidling cursed and threatened the head of
the Hitler Youth who'd brought him some of
these boys as replacement troops.)*

What do they want? — to make me out a Frenchman
Spouting: honor, honor? A preacher? Philosopher?
That's someone else's job; I specialize. Morality
Isn't in my line. When the time came, I sold
My honor; I took the oath to Hitler and I fought
His wars, just or unjust, fair means or foul.
I'm here to fight, not save our culture, not make peace,
Not any of those lies we throw around. And I don't
Mind fighting over things that we can't win —
What's lost already, like Berlin; I fight.
I trained for war, get paid, gained my rank
In battle. Damned little else ignites my wires.
I don't screw my friends' wives. I don't rob
Cripples or lead 14-year old soldiers. Not much
Of a decalogue, but that's the best I've got.
Dear God, when my voice is the loudest voice
For decency, I say we're in trouble.

HEINRICH · HIMMLER
REICHSFUEHRER · SS
FORMER · COMMANDER
ARMY · GROUP · VISTULA

· 15 · APRIL · 1945 ·

(A trainload of Lebensborn children, many stolen from families in the East or illegitimate children of SS men, has mistakenly gone to Army HQ at Zossen, 20 miles south of Berlin. MM=72.)

ARYAN · PURITY · A · STRAIN · OF · GOOD ·
BLOOD · THATS · ALL · WE · ASK · YET · IT ·
CARRIES · WITH · IT · SUCH · ENORMOUS ·
DANGERS · WE · MUST · MAKE · SURE · OUR ·
ENEMIES · DONT · GET · A · DROP · OF · IT ·

FOR · ALL · NORDIC · BLOOD · OUR · FOES ·
GET · WILL · GROW · UP · & · NEVER · LEARN
HUMANE · VALUES · WONT · DEVELOP · OUR
INTEREST · IN · CULTURE · BEAUTY · AND
JUSTICE · SUCH · BLOOD · MUST · NEVER ·

KNOW · ITS · PAST · THIS · SHIPMENT · OF
LEBENSBORN · CHILDREN · OUT · OF · OUR
MATERNITY · HAVEN · IN · THE · TAUNUS ·
NEVER · MUST · FALL · INTO · THE · HANDS
OF · THE · RUSSIANS · OR · THE · WESTERN

POWERS · WE · NEED · THEM · TO · FULFILL
QUOTAS · FOR · OUR · NEW · ARMIES · & · TO
REPLACE · ALL · THE · JEWS · GYPSIES · &
SLAVS · WEVE · HAD · TO · WEED · OUT · OF ·
THE · HUMAN · GARDEN · THESE · ARE · NO ·

UKRAINIANS · OR · KASHUBS · THEY · ARE
VALUABLE · BIG · BLOND · & · BLUE - EYED
WHEN · YOU · HELD · INSPECTION · THERE
YOU · ALWAYS · FOUND · THEM · FRESH · AS
ZINNIAS · IN · A · WELL - SELECTED · BED

ANYONE • WHO • DARES • UNDERTAKE • TO •
BUILD • A • HEALTHY • ORDERLY • BENIGN
CULTURE • WILL • NATURALLY • HAVE • TO
DESTROY • A • FEW • CULLS • THESE • OUR •
ELECTED • CHILDREN • WILL • FINALLY •

FORGET • THEIR • PARENTS • ONCE • THEY
GUESS • THAT • THEIR • OWN • SURVIVAL •
HINGES • ON • IT • WE • CAN • CONSTANTLY
INSIST • THAT • THOSE • PARENTS • WERE
JAILBIRDS • WHORES • ETC • SO • WE • CAN

KEEP • THEM • LOYAL • BESIDES • THEYD •
LIVE • LIKE • PRINCES • THE • TRAINED •
MASTERS • OF • THIS • EARTH • EVEN • SO •
NOT   ALL   OF   THEM • MAY • APPRECIATE
OUR • EFFORTS • TO • SAVE • THEM • FROM •

PARENTS • OF • FAULTY • BLOOD • I • JUST
QUAKE • TO • THINK • THAT • SOME • MIGHT
REVERT • TO • OLD • FEELINGS • OR • DEAD
STANDARDS • WE • HAVE • TO • RECOGNIZE
THE • RISKS • DEMANDED • TO • FOUND • A •

UTOPIA • JUST • THINK • CONSIDER • THE
VENGEANCE • FOR • THEIR • KIN • THEYD •
WREAK • ON • US • IN • NO • MORE • THAN • 20
YEARS • WE • MUST • RUSH • THEM • OUT • OF
ZOSSEN • OR • "DISINFECT" • THEM • NOW

III

16 APRIL 1945
THE RUSSIAN ATTACK

CHORUS

LEADER: Old Lady Barkeep's radio told
The gospel truth as good as gold;
    Still, something made you nervous —
Not that you'd doubt a German's word
But nearly all Berliners heard
    The BBC Overseas Service.

BBC: 16 April 1945. Before dawn this morning, the largest artillery barrage ever mounted in the East led off the Red attack on Berlin. Even the Russian gunners were shaken by the concussion as blood ran from their ears.

RADIO BERLIN: Dr. Goebbels assures all Berliners that our seasoned troops and heavily armored units are sworn to die before yielding one inch of ground.

BBC: In many sectors, Red Army assault troops encountered only Home Guard platoons of grandfathers and boys under fifteen years of age.

RADIO BERLIN: It is now that our High Command, some of history's finest military minds, will reveal their true mettle.

BBC: Elsewhere, despite the Germans' lack of fuel, ammunition or equipment, some veteran units showed a surprising willingness to sacrifice their lives.

RADIO BERLIN: Once more, our leaders will display that same unwavering devotion to Folk and Fuehrer they have always shown.

BBC: Allied commanders appealed to the people of Berlin to give up this senseless struggle, to save their city with all the refugees and wounded, the helpless wives and children in it.

RADIO BERLIN: The German soldier stands firm as ever. If, however, certain treacherous or cowardly elements dare rise among us....

BBC: All civilian and military personnel not guilty of actual war crimes are guaranteed an honorable capitulation....

RADIO BERLIN: Already "flying squads" of loyal SS soldiers are meting out summary justice to all traitors and deserters. Those who even speak of surrender....

BBC: We are at war only with those leaders who have involved your nation in crimes against humanity, then have abandoned you to suffer for their acts.

RADIO BERLIN: Know that Our Fuehrer has chosen to remain here in Berlin at the head of his valiant forces. He stands always beside you in this struggle....

CHO:	Have our Leaders gone South?
LEADER:	Wouldn't you?
CHO:	Do the Reds fire on white flags?
LEADER:	The SS do.
CHO:	Who can we surrender to?
LEADER:	To the lamppost. To the noose.

COL. GEN. GOTTHARD HEINRICI
COMMANDER, ARMY GROUP VISTULA

— 16 April 1945.

*(The main Soviet attack is against Berlin,
not Prague as Hitler had insisted. Against his
orders, Heinrici uses an old ruse to save his
advance troops.)*

I have not actually withdrawn from our
Front line positions. It just so happens
No men are in them at the moment.
So then: the Russian gunners waste
Artillery on our empty foxholes,
Abandoned gun emplacements. They finance
Our new installations, blast out
New foxholes, more places for a man
To hide. When this barrage stops, we'll
See who gets there first, moves back in,
Preparing a warm welcome for them.
I have not actually retreated. I have
Obeyed orders — my own way. The art
Of winning battles without troops, with
Empty positions, empty rifles, empty
Promises. You can't say I'm not acting
In the Fuehrer's own spirit. It all has
A certain Bohemian corporal's flare to it.

(Secretly negotiating with the West, Himmler rehearses the protocol of surrender. MM=76.)

A · SIMPLE · HANDSHAKE · THAT · WOULD ·
BE · BEST · WE · MILITARY · MEN · SHARE ·
COMMON · SYMPATHIES · & · SO · WE · CAN ·
DISPENSE · WITH · SOME · FORMALITIES
EVEN · PRAISE · HIS · STRATEGY · POSE ·

FOR · PHOTOGRAPHS · TOGETHER · WITH ·
GROUPS · OF · ALLIED · OFFICIALS · AND
HIGH · BRASS · THEN · WE · CAN · SETTLE ·
INTO · DISCUSSIONS · ON · PRESERVING
JUSTICE · & · ORDER · IN · EUROPE · & · ON

KEEPING · THE · REDS · BACK · OF · FIXED
LINES · HIS · FRIENDS · CALL · HIM · IKE
MAYBE · BETTER · NOT · PERHAPS · OFFER
NOTHING · BUT · A · STIFF · BOW · UNBEND
ONLY · TO · A · SMILE · NOT · UNFRIENDLY

PERHAPS · A · FULL · MILITARY · SALUTE
QUICK · NEAT · CASUAL · NOTHING · OVER
REHEARSED · AND · NOT · INTIMIDATED ·
SUPPOSE · HE · SNUBS · ME · DEMANDS · TO
TAKE · MY · PISTOL · HED · NEVER · BE · SO

UNGRACIOUS · WHAT · TO · SAY · THOUGH ·
VICTORY · IS · YOURS · POOR · GENERALS
WHOSE · STARS · BODE · ILL · MUST · HAIL
YOU · WHOSE · FORTUNES · ARE · AT · THE ·
ZENITH · WHOSE · MERCY · IS · RENOWNED

DR. JOSEPH GOEBBELS
MINISTER FOR PROPAGANDA

— 16 April 1945.

*(In his study, Goebbels destroys diaries and
mementos, among them a photo of himself as
a child.)*

Diaries: since the age of twelve
Books on my conquests lined my shelves —
Ledgers on all the various selves
I've had. Like Don Juan, you begin to
Count up the psyches you've got into.

> *Paul Joseph Goebbels, five years old:*
> *Small body, large head, the eyes cold.*

What's eating you, boy? Clothing? Food?
Your parents gave you all they could;
They cared. *Then,* even your leg was good.
At seven, something sucks the marrow
From your left shin. Too short, too narrow,
That bone goes frail as wingstruts for a sparrow,
Venus' tough little guttersnipe.
You've got to change your stripe, your type,
Change diet, habits, appetite.
That leg won't grow; now, each bite
You fill your gut with feeds your limp.
Your sound parts learn to starve, to scrimp.

> *Dark velvet suit; white lacey collar.*
> *Fit for a parish priest or scholar.*

At first I studied for the priesthood.
No church's doctoring did the least good
Against this mind's sulfuric, spilt
On every edifice they built.

When we talked politics, I'd choose
Whichever side seemed sure to lose;
I'd win. Then I'd switch sides to oust
Every credo I'd just espoused.
I left school, changed my university
Eight times, tried out the full diversity
Of heroes, lovers, fields of study,
Beliefs. Red hot to be somebody,
I wrote a novel and two plays,
Then fifty Socialist essays.
When those got turned down by the Jews,
I chose the one force left to choose:
The far Right. There, I dumped one boss
And tricked the second, quick to cross
And recross lines as the winds veered.
Then, though, all maps changed: He appeared.

> *Paul Joseph Goebbels. So you waited*
> *For gods or heroes who, if they did*
> *Not exist, could be created.*

He came — like manifest pure essence —
To be, not to become. His presence
Hummed all around us, a live source
Circuited with voltaic force.
In his charged field we woke to find
Each random impulse, heart or mind,
Wheeled "About, Face!" then stood aligned.
On the world's flux he stamped a state
Of North, South; good, evil; love, hate.
He showed us how to hate and who —
Turned all bad blood the same way: Jew.

> *Paul Joseph Goebbels at five years:*
> *Too small; yet this whole world fears*
> *Mere atoms whose unstable, fierce*
> *Alterability can shake the spheres.*

We Nazis said the Future was
Well known to those who shared our cause.

My job was building a new Past.
Too bad; not even bygones last.
Once more, we raze our history:
I fuel the flames with my diary
Of twenty-one years. For some twenty-three,
Arrested, single-minded and steadfast,
I've been somebody. The time's passed.
These Russian slaves will set me free
To change myself again and be
Someone they need; if they need none,
I'm free to not be — be no one
Who's true to Nothing. Their will will be done.

REICHSMARSCHALL HERMANN GOERING

—16 April 1945.

(Goering's family lived in a castle owned by Ritter von Epenstein, reportedly Jewish, the mother's lover. He imagines his interrogation by the Allies.)

NAME OF THE PRISONER: Hermann von Epenstein.
TITLE OR OFFICE: The Reich's Master Huntsman,
    Plenipotentiary for the Four Year Plan.
PLACE OF DWELLING: The Castle Veldenstein.
ALIAS OR NICKNAME: The Last Renaissance Man,
    Hitler's Paladin, Proconsul, The Flying Stuntsman.
FAMILY: Son of Fanny Goering, adopted son
    To Ritter von Epenstein, the castle's lord.
DIVERSIONS: Nude dancing, a foxtail at the ass.
ACHIEVEMENTS: I never stopped to record
    Whatever heights I scaled or challenges I won.
INTERESTS: Castles, diamonds, fancy dress.
WAR CRIMES: Liars called me an art thief.
FATE: Successor to the Chief.

PRISONER'S CORRECT NAME: Goering, Hermann.
TITLE: Lieutenant; Commander, First Air Wing
    Or Flying Circus; Successor to the Red Knight.
ALIAS OR NICKNAME: The Iron German.
FAMILY: Son of Fanny and Heinrich Goering,
    Devoted civil servant, able and upright,
    Who cared for his nation, wife and son.
DIVERSIONS: To hang down outside my Albatros
    And photograph gun placements, dead below.
ACHIEVEMENTS: Order of Merit and the Iron Cross.
WAR CRIMES: I have committed none.
INTERESTS: To honor a brave foe
    But fight him hard, fight well and not yield.
FATE: A swift death or the field.

PRISONER IS CALLED: Herr Reaktion.
TITLE AND OFFICES: The Reichsmarschall;
    Interior Minister of Prussia; President
    Of the Reichstag; Reichsminister for Aviation.
PLACE OF DWELLING: The Memorial Karinhall;
    The Minister's Leipzigerstrasse Residence.
FAMILY: Pure, back to the twelfth century:
    The houses Hohenzollern and Wittelsbach,
    By marriage to the Count and Countess Rosen.
INTERESTS: Drinking with officers of good stock;
    Saving friends' jobs despite their inefficiency.
WAR CRIMES: As a boy, doubling my forces, posing
    Toy soldier armies in front of a mirror.
FATE: To fall with my Fuehrer.
IDENTITY: Herr Meier, the homeless Jew.
TITLE: Commander, Luftwaffe; Air Minister.
ALIAS: Pig; Gas Bag; the Barrage Balloon.
FAMILY: The abandoned six-weeks' child, born to
    Fanny Goering, geboren Tiefenbrunn,
    And Heinrich Goering, cuckolded by her,
    Dishonored and neglected by his son.
DIVERSIONS: Weak jokes while bombs fall outside.
ACHIEVEMENTS: Surcease from pain. Otherwise none.
INTERESTS: Men of bad conscience. Paracodeine.
WAR CRIMES: My cities lie in ruins. I supplied
    My men no rations, no ammunition and no hope.
FATE: The lime pit and the rope.

MAGDA GOEBBELS

—16 April 1945.

*(At their villa, Magda lies in bed, pondering
the fate of her six children by Goebbels.)*

You can destroy the evidence
Of what you did or meant to do.
Joseph's burning all documents
That show what skills statesmen employ
To lose their world. You made plans, too.

You can destroy each telltale clue
That you're a Lady with a Past.
If the Present's got tired of you
Like some cheap, played-out Christmas toy,
Right here you hold the Future fast.

You can destroy all power to choose.
You'd be unhappy with one man
As with the next. Still, you could lose
Their loyalty. We take our joy,
Then leave before the others can.

You can destroy men's confidence
That they can always count on you
To take wounds but take no offense;
Your father thought so. You play coy;
You can wipe out your virtues, too.

You can destroy the clemency
That's kept you hopelessly outclassed.
Draw up, then, in cold dignity
To meet your conqueror's envoy:
You'll look down on them all at last.

You can destroy each weakling qualm
That holds you bed-ridden, aghast
At your own thoughts. Rise, calm:
In the end, Helen burnt down Troy.
You, too, once played things loose and fast.

You can destroy, shut down this whole
Dull little drama that you two
Produced and cast. You played your role.
Five pretty girls; one laggard boy:
One great scene still remains for you.

You can destroy everything worth
Stealing from you. Stripped and downcast,
You can leave scarcely this scorched earth
For them, your betters, to enjoy.
These children? They're too good to last.
                    You can destroy.

ADOLF HITLER

— 16 April 1945

(Anticipating his imminent defeat and death,
he contrasts the suicide of his niece and lover,
Geli Raubal, with the surrender of Stalingrad
by Field Marshal Paulus.)

Zhukov's First Front crossing the Oder
On boats, rafts, tree trunks, blocks of wood.

Eight years, my Will was the Given.

"Nothing exists in this movement
But what I wish to exist."

Want and want's fulfillment, one.

Eleven armies thirty-eight miles from Berlin.

Bismarck called politics "the Art of
The Possible." I willed what was not.

Two and one half million men against
Our thousands. One against one hundred.

"Let no man dare say 'This is
Impossible.' Germany must live."

Nothing succeeds so brilliantly as
The Impossible; the World as Will.

Let no man dare say that I willed
This Russian contamination.

What, hidden in my Will, willed
Paulus' collapse, willed Geli's death?

Let no man dare say I ordered
Our best men North, our armor South,
Marked Prague as their major target.

> "We create you, this date, Field Marshal."
> None created in the field before.
> None ever has surrendered.

To fight to the last inch of ground,
To the last man, the last drop of blood.

> "I'll kill myself before I'll live
> Like a prisoner in my room, a slave.
> I have the right to study singing."

Who would accept what is
Is criminal, too vile to exist.

> "Whore. Just hot for some Vienna stud.
> Clear out any time you please. I'm going."

To yield one's life up to a greater purpose,
To our vaster, purer Will.

> "Besides I just can't do those...acts
> You want me to...I get no pleasure...."

To want what no man in this life has:
This life, this excrement...

They'll teach him Death's advantages.

> Even a woman with an ounce of pride.

> "With your pistol. Shot herself."

Death, and with honor, is.

> Her sacrifice that magnifies my
> Immortality, re-enters my containment.

To have known, two long years, this war was lost
And still sleep this morning well past 9 o'clock.

Will Death and you resume dominion:
Their Deaths that mount up to your glory.
Your Death restored to your own Will.

CHORUS: REFUGEES

(Terrified by reports of the Red troops in the East, more than a million refugees passed through Berlin in early 1945. They were permitted to stay there no more than 48 hours.)

Men do what men have done

    Nearer, they're always nearer,
      Right behind us, always.
    Any day, now, soon; they say,
      Frau, komm; Frau, komm.

Longer than histories run;

    Her skirt yanked up
      Over her head;
    Two of them knelt, knees
      Pinning her shoulders

The muddy, rutted road runs on

    One by one by one,
      All that day, that night;
    Laughing, jeering what
      Our troops had done to them.

As roads have gone.

    They dug up a buried
      SS uniform. Every
    Woman there impaled,
      Every man castrated.

Men do what men have done
    Longer than histories run;
The muddy, rutted road runs on
    As roads have gone.

IV

20 APRIL 1945
HITLER'S BIRTHDAY

Old Lady Barkeep's maxims say
If enemy forces march your way
    Be courteous and cautious.
Hitch your belt in two more notches;
Burn uniforms and bury watches;
Then paint your daughter's face in blotches
With small red chancres where her crotch is —
    She'll look too sick and nauseous
To rape or drag off for a whore
Servicing half an army corps.
Meantime, better enjoy the war;
    The peace will be atrocious.

DR. JOSEPH GOEBBELS
MINISTER FOR PROPAGANDA

—19 April 1945

(At his villa, Goebbels empties papers from his desk into the fireplace. Partially crippled since childhood, he had had many casual affairs, especially with actresses. Earlier that day, he had sent away his aged mother whose firm faith he had always envied and admired.)

East Prussia, Silesia, Norway —
We're getting good at loss. Today,
My country house fell. Soon, we'll be
Preaching desert philosophy.

BERLIN'S DEFENDER
STRIPS FOR ACTION

Mementos. Who ever would have thought
I'd own so much? Still, you get caught
Wanting things.

[takes a packet of letters]

Anka — my first lover.
I pissed away months, moping over
That fool.
Elsa — she called me "Stropp."
But that time I came out on top
And dropped her first.

[drops these, then many others, in the fire]

The trash! You get
Possessed with ownership.

And yet
My foot spared me the worst excess.
You learn that you can live on less
When you can't grow. You can still change
Your shape, your loyalties; estrange
Your past — friends, family, lover,
Heroes, beliefs.

[picks up the photograph of a beautiful woman]

Lida Baarova.
Lida Baarova.

[puts it back; takes other papers]

What a loss
To us — Gregor Strasser, my old boss.
And Ernst Roehm. You can't help make friends.
Things you'll just have to turn against.

NAZIS DUMP STRASSER
ESCAPES TO ITALY

[burns these; takes others]

Actresses — they live to change roles.
You don't ask them to pledge their souls
To one part. So, they come; they go.
There's no one there you'd care to know.

[takes Baarova's picture again]

Baarova. Liduschka. There
Is one beautiful woman. You'd care
Where she's gone. If you knew. We kept clear
One phone line, so each of us could hear
The other breathe. When he forbid

Us to each other...I really did
Think I could be faithful. Desire
Deludes a man.

[tears the picture across]

So. In the fire.
But after things like that, you want.
You try suits, women, cars; you haunt
The nightclubs and the theatre;

NAZI WHORELORD
COUNTS CONQUESTS

You buy up paintings, furniture,
Plates, silver, glass. You can't help start
Hankering to keep some small part
Of this world. You wear satins, ermine,
Rouge and rings, gross as Fat Hermann.

𝔅𝔢𝔥𝔬𝔩𝔡 a camel 𝔰𝔥𝔞𝔩𝔩
more 𝔢𝔞𝔰𝔦𝔩𝔶 𝔭𝔞𝔰𝔰 . . .

*[goes to the French window and looks
out at the lights of Berlin burning]*

Now we can get down to what
Counts — cleaning out the whole vile lot.
Ernst Roehm was right: only a man
Who has no possessions can
Afford ideals. We learn once more
To do without. Where but in war —
The leveler — do all things meet?
Rich and poor, now, dig in the street
Together; walls bombed out, in flame.
Bury weak men and strong the same.

𝔗𝔥𝔢 race 𝔦𝔰 not to 𝔱𝔥𝔢 𝔰𝔴𝔦𝔣𝔱
nor 𝔱𝔥𝔢 battle to 𝔱𝔥𝔢 𝔰𝔱𝔯𝔬𝔫𝔤

[goes to the piano]

EDUCATION MINISTER
PLAYS GERMAN SONGS

[plays and sings]

We've got to go off to the wars,
  And who knows when, my brothers?
We march out through the gates of town—
  Farewell, both Father and Mother.

Farewell, both Father and Mother. Today
I sent my poor old mother away.

[takes her picture from the piano]

FAREWELL TO THE PEASANT MOTHER
WHOSE SIMPLE FAITH INSPIRED HIM

Old and poor? Yes. As sure and steady
As she ever was. And ready
For what comes. Neither one would let
Me give them one red cent. Yet, yet
They scratched and scrimped years, just to get
My first piano. So I could
Have something. Almost as good.

It was your clear faith that drove me through the world. But I had
the Midas touch. In my fingers everything turned smoke — beliefs, creeds,
faiths. You never reproached me, though you must have wondered at the
life we led.
  Go. Take the time that's left you. It is right: you can believe. I doubt.
I doubt.

𝕷𝖊𝖆𝖛𝖊 𝖇𝖔𝖙𝖍 𝖋𝖆𝖙𝖍𝖊𝖗 𝖆𝖓𝖉
𝖒𝖔𝖙𝖍𝖊𝖗 𝖆𝖓𝖉 𝖋𝖔𝖑𝖑𝖔𝖜 𝖆𝖋𝖙𝖊𝖗 𝖒𝖊

[breaks her picture and throws it in the fire]

Ho! Clubfoot Joe, the Boche warlord
Comfortably seated at the keyboard;
Your Emperor Zero now returns
To tickle the keys while Berlin burns.

[plays and sings again]

The nutmeg flowers are lovely;
    The cloves are sharp and sweet.
Now comes the time of parting
    Never again to meet.

The winter's snows are melting;
    Far off these streams will flow.
Now out of my sight you vanish;
    Out of my thoughts you go.

[gets up]

Out of sight, out of mind. We're purer,
Rid of her. What's left now? My Fuehrer,
My used wife, the daughters, and one
Partially retarded son.
Flimsy enough, these ties of mine.
Tonight, we break off one more line
That lashed us to this pit of violence.

[closes the piano]

No more songs. We must practice silence.

ALBERT SPEER
ARMAMENTS MINISTER

—19 April 1945.

*(Speer arrives to ask Hitler to save Berlin by
surrendering it as an open city. Before going
down the Bunker steps, he stops in the Chan-
cellery.)*

Paul,
My old
Schoolmate,
My own doctor —
Last week I was there.
Propped in his armchair;
No nurse. The needle, used,
By his armrest. Talking, smoking;
Our most acute diagnostic mind. What
He would have seen at first glance in his
Patients, he can explain away, can talk it all

To
Death.
He who once
Told us all he
Himself would die by
Cancer, now he describes
All this once more and he sees
Nothing. Nothing. Well, so he may
Escape the guns, escape acknowledging
What it is his cells have been preparing,
Step, by step, in darkness, beyond all control.

Down there, they'll be talking strategy, talking
of miracles. Dry spit on his lips, he will
lurch up off the table shaking worn-out
maps, quote his latest falsified
reports, assign forces wiped
out months ago, supplies
we never had, shriek
at the generals
for merciless
revenge,
for,

As
For me,
I will be
Talking, asking
Him to spare the city —
Meaning let this city fall —
Telling him that I have obeyed and
Scorched this earth of all that could
Support an enemy. Or our people. Perhaps
I should have asked myself whether I'll come back
Up these steps alive. Or maybe, better
Not to know. Better not.

HEINRICH • HIMMLER
REICHSFUEHRER • SS

• 2 0 • A P R I L • 1 9 4 5 •

(At his SS sanatorium, Hohenlychen, Himm-
ler frets: he must attend Hitler's birthday cer-
emony but Count Bernadotte of the Swedish
Red Cross waits at Himmler's estate to ar-
range surrender of his forces. MM=80.)

```
ALMOST • ENOUGH • TO • DRIVE • YOU • MAD
BELIEVE • ME • SMALL • WONDER • IF • THE
CHIEFS • GONE • MAD • GOOD • LORD • DONT
DARE • EVEN • THINK • SUCH • THOUGHTS •
EVERYONE • PULLING • AT • ME • ALL • DAY

FOR • PITYS • SAKE • KERSTEN • SAYS • TO
GIVE • UP • ALL • JEWS • TO • THE • SWEDES
HITLER • DEMANDS • EVERY • CAMP • JEWS
INMATES • GUARDS • BLOWN • UP • WHY • I •
JUST • CANT • NOT   WHEN  I'VE   GOT   TO

KEEP • MY • GOOD • NAME • IN • THE • WEST •
LITTLE • ENOUGH • THEY • WORRY • ABOUT
MY • PROBLEMS • CAN • WE • LET • SOME • GO
NO • KALTENBRUNNER • KEEPS • HIS • EYE
ON • EVERY • MOVE • WELL • SUPPOSE • WE •

PERHAPS • JUST • MARCHED • THEM • ALL •
QUIETLY • AWAY • SOMEWHERE • TO • THE •
REAR • MOST • OF • THEM • WEAK • ALREADY
SICK • NO • SUPPLIES • HOW • FAR • COULD
THEY • GET • EVERY • ROAD • STRAFED • BY

U • S • PLANES • YET • THE • CHIEF • WOULD
VERY • PROBABLY • SEE • THROUGH • THAT
WHAT • ARE • JEWS • EVER • BUT • A • TRIAL
YOU • CAN • SEE • HOW • WE • CAME • TO • TRY
ZYKLON • B • BUT • THERES • NOT • ENOUGH

ALSO • SCHELLENBERG • WONT • LET • YOU
BE • ALWAYS • SAYING • ITS • OUR • LAST •
CHANCE • FOR • SOME • SORT • OF • ACTION
DEPOSE   HIM • OR • PERSUADE • HIM • ITS
ESSENTIAL • HE • RESIGN • HIS • OFFICE
```

FOR • THE • NATIONS • GOOD • WHY • DEAR •
GOD • HED • START • IN • YELLING • AT • ME
HAVE • ME • SHOT • DEAD • ON • THE • SPOT •
I • DONT • KNOW • WHY • THEY • CANT • ALL •
JUST • LEAVE • ME • ALONE • HOW • DO • YOU

KNOW • WHAT • LOOKS • MORE • HONORABLE
LOOK • NOW • I • COULD • GO • THERE • WITH
MY • BEST • MEN • YOU • CANT • TAKE • GUNS
NEVERTHELESS • A • SURPRISE • ATTACK
OUR • DOCTORS • COULD • DIAGNOSE • IT •

PARKINSONS • DISEASE • THAT • SHOULD
QUIET • THE • MASSES • THEN • WE • MUST •
REACH • EISENHOWER • YET • HOW • MANY •
S • S • DOCTORS • WOULD • HELP • YOU • OUT
THE • COWARDS • NEVER • WOULD • SPEAK •

UP • TRY • AS • WE • MIGHT • TO • INSTILL •
VALUES • COURAGE • SELF-SACRIFICE •
WHY • DIDNT • I • LAY • PLANS • FOR • THIS
YEARS • AGO • WHY • LET • THOSE • GRADE •
Z • IDIOTS • BOTCH • IT • ON • JULY • 20TH

AND • YET • NINE • MONTHS • THAT • MUST •
BE • SIGNIFICANT • LETS • GET • A • STAR
CHART • ON • IT • NINE • MONTHS • TO • THE
DAY • A • PREGNANT • PERIOD • SINCE • HE
ELUDED • STAUFFENBERGS • BOMB • AND •

FLUMMOXED • THE • GENERALS • REVOLT •
GOOD • HEAVENS • IF • WE • HAVENT • HAD •
HORRIFYING • PROBLEMS • EVER • SINCE
IVE • DRAGGED • THEM • INTO • COURT • OR
JUST • LIQUIDATED • THOSE • FEW • THAT

KNEW • MY • PART • IN • IT • BY • NOW • THAT
LEAVES • ME • FEW • FRIENDS • YET • HOW •
MUCH • HELP • WOULD • SUCH • ALLIES • BE
NOW • COULD • WE • GET • MEASUREMENTS •
ON • HIS • SKULL • WE • COULD • POSSIBLY

```
PROVE • HES • A • JEW • THE • WEST • COULD
QUELL • THE • RED • THREAT • WED • GO • ON
RESTORING • ORDER • HERE • IN • EUROPE
SO • THEN • THIS • BIRTHDAY • CEREMONY
TODAY • YOUVE • GOT • TO • GO • WISH • HIM

UNTOLD • HAPPINESS • UNPRECEDENTED
VICTORY • IF • HE • EVER • FOUND • WHOS •
WAITING • NOW • BACK • AT • YOUR • VILLA
YOURE • ON • YOUR • LAST • TRIP • TO • THE
ZOO • OH • WHAT • TO • DO • TO • DO • TO • DO •
```

ALBERT SPEER
ARMAMENTS MINISTER

—20 April 1945, 2200 hours.

*(Nuremberg and Stuttgart have fallen and
the Ruhr pocket has collapsed. After Hitler's
birthday ceremony, Speer climbs the Bunker
steps into the garden, then travels to Ham-
burg to subvert Hitler's scorched earth policy.)*

Take
A breath.
Take your own
Breath. Even air
That reeks with smoke,
With brick dust, plaster...
Even this darkness, this night
Sky, streaked by searchlights, flaring
With the light of our own buildings burning,
Is better than that man-made manufactured air, than
Artificial man-made light, than plans for rescue, talk
Of miracle weapons, of death rays, than that man-made darkness.

Today, his "birthday party"; all of them come up into the wreckage
of the Chancellery, into these gardens' ruins for one breath.
He shuffles along, his left foot dragging behind him,
pats the boys lined up there on the cheek, pins
his tinny medals on their chests. Then
sends them to be ground up under
tank tread. They beam with
gratitude. He limps a
little more so *they*
will pity *him.*
Lord, how
long?

The
Allied
Bomb fleets
Hold back. Not
At all a good sign;
It may mean ground troops
Are moving in now; the shelling
Sounds heavier than before; more Russian
17.5s hauled up here from the Silesian front.
So, the Ruhr gone, lost to us; Silesia lost to us
This last time. Yes, lost for good. Mines, power plants,
All our best installations lost.... And is that all? Is that all?

He has broken his word: he will defend the city, street by street.
That is, destroy the city, street by street. He will not go
see the cities, our casualties, our refugees, Goebbels'
photos, the officers, the reports Heinrici sends in
from the Silesian front. Irrelevant. But to
what? And is that all? So he neglects
His knowing. At least I drove out
to Silesia. At Rybnik, mine
crews switching over
for the Russians;
Kattowitz, no
doubt....

Last night, again, my dreams came out
of Käthe Kollwitz: *The Guillotine.*
That murderous dance — the mob half-
crazed, killing off its rulers.

What was it
Hanke saw there in the East?
And warned me not
to find out, not to see? What
are the Russians digging up?
the sort of things
I saw in the camps —
forced labor, wretched conditions...

He lets
me live; why?
Time for a cigarette.
He forbids us all to smoke
then sends us all up the chimney.
(What chimney? Where?) **Idiot, use your**
eyes. If he has his way we won't have one
chimney standing. And does he neglect his knowing
I did not and I will not obey him? He may well know I
am going out to betray him. **Too certainly, he knows that I**
am faithful. **Knows that I** evade my better self. **Knows that I**
neglect my knowing. That he and I, together, we **neglect our knowing.**

REICHSMARSCHALL HERMANN GOERING

—20 April 1945.

*(After Hitler's birthday ceremony, and with
the Russians only a only a few miles away,
Goering prepares to blow up the Karinhall,
his memorial to his first wife whose ardent
mysticism had helped draw him to the Na-
zis.)*

Tell us, dear Reichsmarschall, what seems
The difference between you and Hitler?
*Now that it's fallen, he's content
To detonate the continent;
I'll blow up something pure but littler —
This bastion for ethereal dreams.*

You said your Brown Shirts were like beefsteaks?
They're brown outside; still Red within.
Then does Berlin's fate coincide
With this hall's? *Both have Reds outside;
But Eva Braun's inside Berlin.
This housed my noble Karin's keepsakes.*

Kindly point out the difference, then,
Between Miss Braun and your dear Karin.
*His blond cow started a Braun Movement;
My Karin sparked my mind's improvement
Toward her clear faith — lighter than air and
Volatile as hydrogen.*

Could it be, dear sir, that such high-powered
Ideas are like a zepellin?
*Fly high and you can still come down
In a cowpile — which may be brown
But you're red-faced.* What if you've been
Stalwart.... *The clods still call you coward.*

Are you, then, and your whole Air Force
Like a ballooning currency?
Both our figures did get inflated;
Our thrust and flow turned constipated....
Why not try strict economy
And self-denial? *Too late.* Of course.

Enemies; enemas — much the same?
Both rid you of collected matter.
Well, enemas and combat fronts?
Maybe. But to take two at once
Would take a fatter ass and fatter
Head than mine. You lose all aim.

Could lignite be much like cheese rarebits?
Are either one like drug addiction?
Shoot up or blow up, wide or high;
Till you think you engross the sky....
(That may not be your last conviction.)
Bubbles break easier than habits.

Are soccerballs like an ideal?
You pump them full of emptiness;
Boot them around until they soften;
Shove down that handle once too often,
Though...

> *[pushes down the detonator handle;*
> *the building crumples and collapses]*

What's left you can still depress?
Yourself. You come down to what's real.

DR. JOSEPH GOEBBELS
MINISTER FOR PROPAGANDA

—20 April 1945.

*(Soviet artillery is firing into parts of Berlin.
The previous evening, Goebbels had recorded
a birthday tribute to Hitler which Radio Ber-
lin played on this date.)*

I've known strange loves. When I was young
Many a smooth, Romantic tongue
Slipped through my lips. Later I mastered
My native speech, the surly, bastard
Idiom of our harsh North German.
I spoke; each godless, hellfire sermon
Clinched my possession on these vermin.

Just last year at the Sportpalast,
I diddled thousands to one vast
Insane, delirious orgasm;
Stone cold, my mind controlled each spasm,
Teased them so high, so hot and mad
That they'd take everything I had
To give them. They could only roar
"Ja!" and "Ja!" and "Ja!" once more,
Begging me: let them have it — total war.

We pant for, but we're scornful of,
What we can screw. If we want love,
We lie. In politics, in bed,
We learn the cant that can be said,
The facts that can't. Last night I made
My final radio tirade:
A tribute for the Chief's birthday —
Just think how much I dared not say:

Never before did matters stand on
Never before did a master abandon
A razor's edge so cruel as this;
A nation's crazed fools to the abyss
Still, the majesty of these dark times
Till pride, false strategy and stark crimes
Finds its true essence in our Fuehrer.
Make senseless ruin each hour surer.

We owe our thanks to Him alone
If Russian tanks break stone from stone
Our own dear homeland still stands fast
Blown down by shellburst or bomb blast
And the radiant culture of the West
While raping, killing, laying waste,
Is not yet swallowed by the pit.
Benighted hordes swarm over it.

If our Folk still believe in Him
Who'd choke their lives off from mere whim
And He still stands by His deep vow,
To strangle, starve or hang them now,
That means we've won true victory
We've mined new depths of idiocy
Which may inspire an age unborn;
With mad desires, blind rage and scorn

Our spirit must come to birth again
That spurs blood lust in earthly men
A phoenix rising from its own ashes
To finish things as this world crashes
From the rubble of temporary loss;
Tumbling them in their burial foss.
Over the ruins that vandals burned
Our people's noble aims will have returned.
These stunted cripples who have learned
Nothing except how vile a death they've earned.

It's their own rage and greed they must
Blame for post-coital disgust;
It was their hankerings, not mine,
That turned their "Ja!" into my "Nein!"
Now, when their little throats get cut,
I say, demand me nothing. What
You know, you know; what you've heard, heard.
Henceforth, I never will speak word.

Today we played His birthday farce,
Wished Him great joy, then licked His arse.

ADOLF HITLER

—20 April 1945, 1900 hours.

*(After his birthday ceremony, Hitler with-
draws to his sitting room where he holds one
of Blondi's puppies. Lines from Lohengrin
surface in his thoughts.)*

Best stuffed in a bag and drowned.
This mockery: my best bitch
Pregnant once she can't survive.

The man will lie on his back; he is, of course, completely naked.

My Effie's sister knocked up
By Fegelein. Luck lets me off of
One humiliation: I breed no child.

His partner will crouch over his head or chest, as he prefers.

Pisspot generals whining for surrender:
Their cities, populations, lives.
Party maggots offering me presents;
Careful not to wish me a long life —
Their one shortcoming I can share.

She may remove, perhaps, only her underthings. Exposed suddenly, the
private parts can yield an exquisite shock and pleasure.

Cub, in Landsberg Prison, my flowers
Filled three prison rooms. The faithful
Sang beside me in my cell. I unwrapped
Presents, cut my cake. We laughed:
What? — no file inside it?

The cake my mother made me.... No....

She will present, most frequently, her back.

That's Edmund's, my brother's cake.
But I ate his. I spit on what was left.

The Prison Governor's little daughter,
Like this, curled up on my lap.

She must not start at once; he must ask, beg her, to begin.

Oh, we hear their song:
Live on. Live longer. Don't leave us
To the Russian gunners. Save us;
Lead us to the mountains.

𝕺𝔥 𝔰𝔱𝔞𝔶! 𝕯𝔬𝔫'𝔱 𝔩𝔢𝔞𝔳𝔢 𝔲𝔰 𝔥𝔢𝔯𝔢 𝔣𝔬𝔯𝔰𝔞𝔨𝔢𝔫;
𝕺𝔲𝔯 𝔪𝔢𝔫 𝔞𝔯𝔢 𝔴𝔞𝔦𝔱𝔦𝔫𝔤 𝔣𝔬𝔯 𝔱𝔥𝔢𝔦𝔯 𝔉𝔲𝔢𝔥𝔯𝔢𝔯.

Even the zoo beasts, my old neighbors, pacing
Till their keeper brings the perfect gift:
One lead pellet. A man who would accept
What is, is criminal, too vile to live.

He will grovel on the floor, declaring himself unworthy to touch her
shoes, even to live.

Two flights, today, to the garden. Schoolboys:
Lined up like graves. Hands I have to touch.

It is not the mere fact of the urine or faeces that matters.
Rather, he must be able to watch as these emerge into existence.

Back up again to Berchtesgaden?
The locked elevator lurching through
Dead rock in the mountain side?
Come out over traitorous cities, lecherous
Faces, Jews with blond hair, blue eyes, who'd
Steal our birthright, pull us down to slime.

She must now show disgust; may revile him, even kick at him.

My pills; Morrell's injections.
My cake, chairs, rugs — without them,
Bare concrete. Same as any
Jew degenerate at Auschwitz.

        Edmund died though, my brother,
        When I was eleven. His birthday
        Would have been eight days ago.

Only when he is fully excited by his own demands, may she release her
urine, open her bowels. The danger of taking this substance in his mouth
should heighten his excitement.

        She'd lost three others. She, only
        She, was glad I had survived.

Live on; only live. Don't
Leave us to the loneliness,
The spoiling of affections.

        He kept me in. But she,
        She made a special cake for me —

Over and over, I've said they could
Survive: overcome the facts.

        Only the two of us together.

Now he should achieve his climax, alone and without assistance.

        Our old Fighters — that was comradeship.
        You have Blondi's underside. My diet cook,
        My secretaries — they know how to listen.
        Namesake, cub, you've done your month
        In this filth. My cake; I'll eat it, too.

𝕿𝖍𝖊 𝕲𝖗𝖆𝖎𝖑 𝖆𝖑𝖗𝖊𝖆𝖉𝖞 𝖈𝖆𝖑𝖑𝖘 𝖎𝖙𝖘 𝖜𝖆𝖓𝖉𝖊𝖗𝖊𝖗!

When he has washed and begged forgiveness, she may embrace and com-
fort him.

My birthday present, my file: my
Cartridge of pure cyanide. Crawl back
Into the cave, work down in dry leaves...

Or she may lie down at his side.

An old dog deciding to lie down.

V

22 – 23 APRIL 1945
IDENTITIES

CHORUS: OLD LADY BARKEEP

Old Lady Barkeep knew the score
On how to tell you've lost a war:
    Everyone's fled who dares;
You find you're executing more
    Of your own men than theirs.

Captured, your guns fire back at you;
The news also — at least what's true —
    Comes from your enemies.
Without much gas, your tanks have slowed
And if they crush things in their road,
    It's your own refugees.

Your rulers order you: stand fast
To the last bullet, the last man, the last
    Drop of blood; fight on!
Then when some foe looms into sight
And you look up for orders, Shite!
    The SOBs are gone.

MAGDA GOEBBELS

—22 April 1945.

(With Soviet tanks in the suburbs, Goebbels'
family has moved into an upper level of the
Bunker.)

i

How can you do the things you know you'll do? —
One last act to bring back integrity.
I've got just one desire left: to be true.

You can't pick how you'll live. Our times will screw
Your poor last virtues from you, ruthlessly.
How can you do the things you know you'll do?

My mother drove me on: get married to
Quandt. Rich. Kind enough. If elderly.
I've got just one desire left: to be true.

He turned me against Friedlander, the Jew —
My stepfather who'd raised me lovingly.
How can you do the things you know you'll do?

Quandt trapped me with young Ernst. He planned to sue
Till I found his old tax books. And the key.
I've got just one desire left: to be true.

Those thin books brought me in the revenue
For leisure, for the best society.
How can you do the things you know you'll do?

And then I heard Him speak: our Leader, who
Might have been talking to no one but me.
I've got just one desire left: to be true
Till death to Him. And what I know I'll do.

How can you live through what life brings you to?
Who's showed us, ever, the least loyalty?
All of us find it hard just to be true.

The Chief was wild for me; yet we all knew
He couldn't marry — He needs to be free.
How can you live through what life brings you to?

They said why not take Joseph, then, in lieu;
The Chief would visit our place secretly.
All of us find it hard just to be true.

Joseph said *he'd* play false. But he came through;
He kept that single promise faithfully.
How can you live through what life brings you to?

I, too, found lovers, given time. Some few
Were his good friends — his staff, his ministry.
All of us find it hard just to be true.

He wanted Lida; I took Karl. Then who
But the Chief sealed us shut — a family!
How can you live through what life brings you to?

So now I won't leave Joseph; I'll die, too.
The children? They'll just have to come with me.
All of us find it hard just to be true
Till death to all this false world brings you to.

The children? They'll just have to come with me.
At their age, how could they find their own way?
We must preserve them from disloyalty.

They're too good for the world we all foresee.
If they were old enough, we know they'd say
It's right and just they'll have to come with me.

My father left — divorced — when I was three.
So how could I leave them alone today?
We must preserve them from disloyalty.

They've been the fist behind my policy
Since Joseph and that Slav girl ran astray;
It's right and just they'll have to come with me.

I slammed his door on him. "Of course you're free.
It's time they learned who cares and who'll betray."
We must preserve them from disloyalty.

My father came: he said Joseph would be
Ruin to us all. I turned him away.
It's right and just they'll have to come with me.

He begged to visit them. He will not see
Them till he dies. That's just the price he'll pay.
We must preserve them from disloyalty
And this false world. They'll have to come with me.

iv

You try to spare them the worst misery;
Who knows what cold force they'd be subject to?
How could we let them fall to treachery,

Disgrace, to brute foes? At the best, they'd see
Scorn in the face of every Red or Jew.
You try to spare them the worst misery.

In evil days, models of constancy
Are the one thing that will still see men through.
How could we let them fall to treachery

When they've once known our Leader? Yet if He,
If we go, just how many could stay true?
You try to spare them the worst misery

Of wanting this, that. From our own past, we
Know things they might have to say or do.
How could we let them fall to treachery,

To making base terms with an enemy,
Denying us and our best ideals, too?
You try to spare them the worst misery,

But they'd still want to live. What if they'd be
Happy — they could prove all we thought untrue.
How could we let them fall to treachery
And their own faults? You end their misery.

DR. JOSEPH GOEBBELS
MINISTER FOR PROPAGANDA

—22 April 1945.

*(Partly to counteract Hitler's hysteria,
Goebbels has moved to the Bunker's lowest
level, opposite to Hitler's room.)*

Stand back, make way, you mindless scum,
Squire Voland the Seducer's come —
Old Bock from Babelsberg whose tower
Falls silent now, whose shrunken power
For lies or lays comes hobbling home
Into this concrete catacomb.

Here's Runty Joe, the cunt collector
Who grew to greatness, first erector
Of myths and missions, fibs and fables,
Who pulled the wool then turned the tables:
He piped the tunes and called the dance
Where shirtless countries lost their pants.

Goatfooted Pan, the nation's gander
To whom Pan-Germans all played pander.
The jovial cob-swan quick to cover
Lida Baarova, his check-list lover:
Swellfoot the Tyrant, he could riddle
Men's minds away, hi-diddle-diddle.

Our little Doctor, Joe the Gimp,
Comes back to limpness and his limp:
Hephaistos, Vulcan, the lame smith
Whose net of lies caught one true myth:
His wife, the famous beauty, whored
By numbskull Mars, the dull warlord.

What if I took my little fling
At conquest, at adventuring,
Pried the lid of Pandora's box off —
There's nothing there to bring your rocks off.
I never saw one fucking day
So fine I courted it to stay.

If I got snarled in my own mesh
Of thighs and bellies, who wants flesh?
I never hankered after matter.
Let Hermann swell up, grosser, fatter,
Weighed down by medals, houses, clothing:
They leave me lean, secured in loathing.

As a young man, I pricked the bubble
Of every creed; I saw that rubble
And offered myself the realms of earth
Just to say Yes. But what's it worth?
No thank you, Ma'am. Behold the Ram
Of God: I doubt, therefore I am.

Here I forsake that long pricktease
Of histories, hopes, lusts, luxuries.
I come back to my first Ideal —
The vacancy that's always real.
I sniffed out all life's openings:
I loved only the holes in things.

So strip down one bare cell for this
Lay Brother of the last abyss.
To me, still, all abstractions smell.
My head and nose clear in this cell
Of concrete, this confession booth
Where liars face up to blank truth.

My tongue lashed millions to the knife:
Here, I'll hold hands with my soiled wife.
My lies piped men out, hot to slaughter;
Here, I'll read stories to my daughter
Then hack off all relations, choose
Only the Nothing you can't lose.

Send back this body, fixed in its
Infantile paralysis.
I was born small: I shall grow less
Till I burst into Nothingness,
That slot in time where only pure
Spirit extends, absent and sure.

I am that spirit that denies,
High Priest of Laymen, Prince of Lies.
Your house is founded on my rock:
Truth crows; now I deny my cock.
Jock of this walk, I turn down all,
Robbing my Peter to play Paul.

I give up all goods I possess
To build my faith on faithlessness.
Black Peter, I belie my Lord —
You've got to die to spread the Word.
Now the last act; there's no sequel.
Soon, once more, all things shall be equal.

EVA BRAUN

— 22 April 1945.

(His mistress' small revenges for Hitler's neglect included singing American songs, her favorite being "Tea for Two." Having chosen to die with him in the Bunker, she seemed serene during the last days.)

Tea for two
And two for tea

> I ought to feel ashamed
> Feeling such joy. Behaving like a spoiled child!
> So fulfilled. This is a very serious matter.
> All of them have come here to die. And they grieve.
> I have come here to die. If this is dying,
> Why else did I ever live?

Me for you
And you for me

> We ought to never flaunt our good luck
> In the face of anyone less fortunate —
> These live fools mourning already
> For their own deaths: these dead fools
> Who believe they can go on living...

And you for me
Alone.

> Who out of all of them, officers, ministers,
> These liars that despise me, these empty
> Women that envy me — so they hate me —
> Who else of them dares to disobey Him
> As I dared? I have defied Him to His face
> And He has honored me.

They sneer at me — at my worrying about
Frau Goebbels' children, that I make fairytales
For them, that we play at war. Is our war
More lost if I console these poor trapped rabbits?
These children He would not give me...

A boy for you
A girl for me

They sneer that I should bring
Fine furniture down this dank hole. Speer
Built this bed for me. Where I have slept
Beside our Chief. Who else should have it?
My furs, my best dress to my little sister —
They would sneer even at this; yet
What else can I give her?

Can't you see
How happy we would be?

Or to the baby
She will bear Fegelein? Lechering dolt!
Well, I have given her her wedding
As if it was my own. And she will have
My diamonds, my watch. The little things you
Count on, things that see you through your
Missing life, the life that stood you up.

Nobody near us
To see us or hear us

I have it all. They are all gone, the others —
The Valkyrie; and the old rich bitch Bechstein;
Geli above all. No, the screaming mobs above all.
They are all gone now. He has left them all.
No one but me and the love-struck secretaries —
Traudl, Daran — who gave up years ago.

That I, I above all, am chosen — even I
Must find that strange. I who was always
Disobedient, rebellious — smoked in the dining car,
Wore rouge when he said we mustn't.
When he ordered that poor Chancellor Schuschnigg
Should go hungry, I sent in food.

We won't have it known, dear,
That we own a telephone, dear.

I who joined the Party, I who took Him
For my lover just to spite my old stiff father —
Den Alten Fritz! — and those stupid nuns.
I ran my teachers crazy, and my mother — I
Held out even when she stuck my head in water.
He shall have none but me.

Day will break
And you will wake

We cannot make it through another month;
We follow the battles now on a subway map.
Even if the Russians pulled back —
His hand trembles, the whole left side
Staggers. His marvellous eyes are failing.
We go out to the sunlight less each day. We live
Like flies sucked up in a sweeper bag.

And start to bake
A sugar cake

He forbade me to leave Berchtesgaden,
Forbade me to come here. I tricked
My keepers, stole my own car, my driver Jung.
He tried to scold me; He was too
Proud of me. Today He ordered me to leave,
To go back to the mountain. I refused.

119

I have refused to save my own life and He,
In public, He kissed me on the mouth!

                              For me to take
                              For all the boys to see.

Once more I have won, won out over Him
Who spoke one word and whole populations vanished.
Until today, in public, we were good friends.
He is mine. No doubt
I did only what He wanted; no doubt
I should resent that. In the face
Of such fulfillment? In the face
Of so much joy?

                    Picture you
                    Upon my knee;
                    Tea for two
                    And two for tea...

ALBERT SPEER
ARMAMENTS MINISTER

—23 April 1945.

*(Frankfurt and Cottbus have fallen; Berlin is
nearly encircled. Soviet troops are advancing
into the city. Flying with Lt. Col. von Poser,
Speer lands on Unter den Linden and hails
an army truck to take him to the Bunker.)*

As we
Flew in,
The city like
Something out of
Dante — a City of Dis.
Smoke rolling up, whole blocks
Burned out, walls broken in like
Paper boxes, cracked like egg shells;
The Reichstag, the Kaiser Wilhelm Church,
In ruins, charred. Out near Kyritz, refugees
Jamming the highways, families with carts, women
Hacking at a dead horse.

*[gets out of the truck on Voss Strasse where he passes the
bodies of soldiers hanged on street lamps]*

He sends more gun squads out
onto our streets to hang our own men: Germans hanging
from their lampposts like venison in shops. No;
my lampposts for their Unter den Linden, for
his triumph. Their crime: they saw no
reason they should die now, reason
for more men to die. Is it a
crime to care about this
life? Can't anybody
have enough of
other men's
dying?

Then
Should we
Believe in our
Enemies' propaganda?
Bodies stacked like wood,
Jews herded into sealed rooms,
Strangled, shot, poisoned by gas,
Mass graves, incinerators day and night,
Medical experiments, lampshades of men's skin,
Rooms of women's hair, false teeth? Too absurd
To think of. How could the world not know? Merely
The stench of bodies burning would be strong enough…

When will they hang us to our own
Lampposts?

*[in the garden he encounters the chimney above
the Bunker's air shaft]*

Why let him live? Why let him go on breathing one day
    more, filling the air we breathe with smoke, with
        death's contagion? "If thine eye offend thee,
            pluck it out." I tried once, tried to slip
                that same gas down this air shaft where
                    he takes his breath. Why fail? Why?
                        Yet I could as well cut off my
                            right arm with my left. So
                                this contaminated, this
                                    withered limb that
                                        putrifies our
                                            air…

I let him live, as he has
let me live. No doubt
but each is sick to dying
of each other.

Can nothing make them see?

I even
keep his photograph
he gave me for *my birthday*
on my own desk
under Käthe Kollwitz' guillotine.

Besides, I never reached Kattowitz;
I steered my own staff car into an
army truck's grill. Searing light.
Then, three months of convalescence.
Some kind Fate saved me after all.

And yet his only purpose...

No.
No man
Ever knows
About such things.
We know only how much
Each person knows he knows...

We must keep faith with that

Until the Russians come...

[enters the Bunker]

REICHSMARSCHALL HERMANN GOERING

—23 April 1945.

*(On the only road still open to the South,
Goering drove to Berchtesgaden with a con-
voy of 40 trucks of personal belongings. In
his HQ there, he examines his vast wardrobe
and recalls his once splendid parties.)*

Dear friends, the moment's come to ask
What lies beneath the glittering gear
And costumes that we see displayed
At the Reichsmarschall's masquerade;
Learn who's romanced and danced us here,
Then face the face behind the mask.

Who can adapt to each new role
And change costumes so cunningly
With each day's new conditions that
He wears a lantern on his hat
If he must run downstairs to see
The man who's come delivering coal?

Who steps up now to the forefront
In lebensraum of lederhosen,
A vest roughcut from a deer's pelt
And dagger tucked in his wide belt
To signify himself the chosen
Chief of Reich Forests and the Hunt?

Whose airman's uniform asserts
Clear blue, horizon to horizon,
Like azure skies no enemy
Dares invade; where sometimes we see
Medals like close-drilled stars bedizen
An ever-expanding universe?

Who wears this tent-sized dressing gown
All day, bought forty business suits
So he could change each hour or two
For fear his rank sweat might soak through?
Is this our famous Puss-in-Boots
Or just some knock-down, drag-out clown?

Who flaunts this frilly satin blouse,
These velvet knickerbockers, that
Alluring jacket of green suede;
Who in such fluff and frou-frou played
A true effete aristocrat,
The idle lord of an old house?

Who wears this modern well-ironed version
Of a toga whose loose hem dangles
Over his circular abdomen
Like an Athenian lord or Roman,
But with his nail paint, rouge and bangles
Looks much more like some debauched Persian?

Who, at the Fuehrer's staff confab,
Accused of crimes just short of treason,
Got Hitler's leave to flee Berlin
And drive South, though he stood there in
The smartest fashion note this season:
Chic American olive-drab?

Who wears this thick flesh, layer on layer —
Loose outposts of a weakening heart?
Who seems a one-man population
Explosion, or expanding nation;
But at showdown gives you a start:
He lifts his mask and no one's there.

LT. GEN. HELMUTH "CRUSHER KARL" WEIDLING
COMMANDER, 56th PANZER CORPS

—23 April 1945.

*(The Eastern front is rapidly collapsing.
Falsely accused of absence from his post,
Weidling was condemned to death on April
22. Having cleared his name, he was given
command of Berlin on the 23rd. He leaves
the Fuehrer's office.)*

Why can't I learn: shut your yap; choke
Down the bag of shit they hand you?
Hot off the lines, sentenced to death,
I stormed down here: "What's going on
And why is this I'm to get shot?"
The Fuehrer clutched my hand, named me
Commandant of this whole garbage dump,
Thousands of old women, little girls.
We'll screw the Slavs to death before
We slow them down. If I squeak through,
I can go in chains to Moscow, Lubianka,
The garottes and thumbscrews. In human charity,
Who'll give me one lead slug in the head?

HEINRICH • HIMMLER
REICHSFUEHRER • SS

• 23 • APRIL • 1945 •

(Driving his own car, Himmler tries to leave the Swedish Embassy at Luebeck after meeting with Count Bernadotte. His wife was Marga, his daughter, Puppi. MM=88.)

```
ALWAYS • THE • SAME • DILEMMAS • STUCK
BETWEEN • STOOLS • BALANCING • THESE
COMPETING • LOYALTIES • BUT • ITS • SO
DIFFICULT • TO • SECRETLY • CONTACT •
EISENHOWER • WHEN • MY • OATH • TO • THE

FUEHRER • FORBIDS • THAT • STILL • THE
GOOD • OF • THE • WHOLE • GERMAN • FOLK •
HAS • TO • HAVE • SOME • CONSIDERATION
I • HAVE • TO • DO • 2 • THINGS • AT • ONCE •
JUST • AS • I • HAVE • A • MORAL • DUTY • TO

KEEP • MARGA • AND • PUPPI • ALMOST • IN
LUXURY • BUT • ALSO • NEED • TO • PUT • MY
MISTRESS • HEDWIG • IN • A • SUITABLY •
NICE • SITUATION • WHO • CAN • DO • BOTH
ON • MY • SALARY • IVE • HAD  TO • BORROW

PARTY • FUNDS • FROM • BORMANN • SO • IM
QUITE • AT • HIS • MERCY • WORSE • MARGA
RAGES • AT • ME • WHEN • I • GO • THERE • TO
SEE • MY • DAUGHTER • & • HEDWIG • POUTS
TALK • ABOUT • 2 - FRONT • WARS • THO • IM

UNDER • BORMANNS • THUMB • I • HAVE • A •
VOW • TO • SET • A • MANLY • EXAMPLE • OF •
WHOLESOME • HARD • SELF - DENIAL • NOT
YIELDING • TO • GREED • AS • DO • THOSE •
ZIONIST • SWINE • AND • YET • IVE • BEEN

ABUSED • VILIFIED • DERIDED • & • JUST
BECAUSE • IVE • BEEN • FREE • FROM • ALL
CORRUPTION • WHAT • IF • WE • TOOK • THE
DIRTY • JEWS • EVIL • WEALTH • I • NEVER
ENRICHED • MY • OWN • SELF • BY • EVEN • 1
```

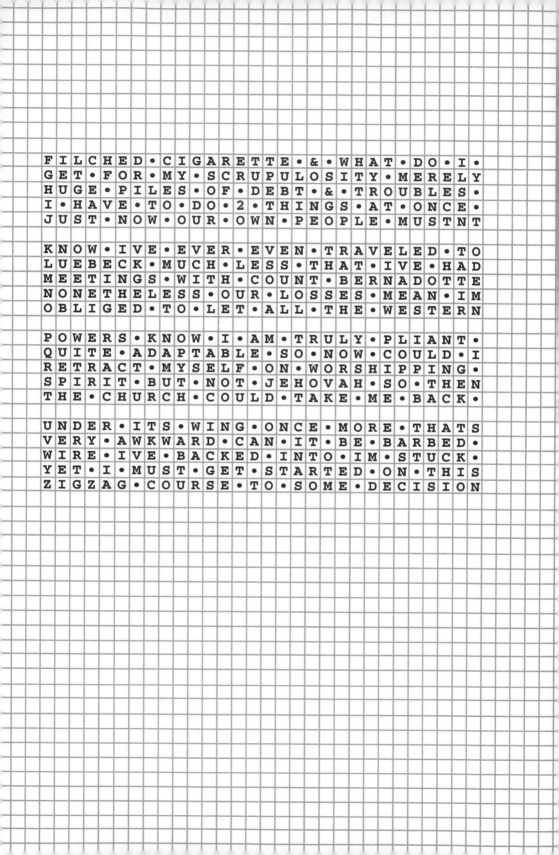

FILCHED • CIGARETTE • & • WHAT • DO • I •
GET • FOR • MY • SCRUPULOSITY • MERELY
HUGE • PILES • OF • DEBT • & • TROUBLES •
I • HAVE • TO • DO • 2 • THINGS • AT • ONCE •
JUST • NOW • OUR • OWN • PEOPLE • MUSTNT

KNOW • IVE • EVER • EVEN • TRAVELED • TO
LUEBECK • MUCH • LESS • THAT • IVE • HAD
MEETINGS • WITH • COUNT • BERNADOTTE
NONETHELESS • OUR • LOSSES • MEAN • IM
OBLIGED • TO • LET • ALL • THE • WESTERN

POWERS • KNOW • I • AM • TRULY • PLIANT •
QUITE • ADAPTABLE • SO • NOW • COULD • I
RETRACT • MYSELF • ON • WORSHIPPING •
SPIRIT • BUT • NOT • JEHOVAH • SO • THEN
THE • CHURCH • COULD • TAKE • ME • BACK •

UNDER • ITS • WING • ONCE • MORE • THATS
VERY • AWKWARD • CAN • IT • BE • BARBED •
WIRE • IVE • BACKED • INTO • IM • STUCK •
YET • I • MUST • GET • STARTED • ON • THIS
ZIGZAG • COURSE • TO • SOME • DECISION

THE GOEBBELS CHILDREN

—23 April 1945.

We wonder how long this will last.
They say it should get over fast,
    Then we can play outside or go
    Back home to see our school friends, so
We wonder how long this will last.

Each of us only brought one toy;
That's strange — for five girls and one boy.
    These are the only clothes we've got
    Down here. Maybe they just forgot
Each of us only brought one toy.

Soldiers come down out of the war;
Haven't they seen young kids before? —
    They stare. We play war with the men
    That live here all the time, but then
Soldiers come down out of the war.

Our sisters shoot at us for fun.
We fall down dead sometimes or run
    Into the radio room and hide.
    Just like the sounds we hear outside,
Our sisters shoot at us for fun.

Our mother stays in bed a lot
And doesn't feel right. Though she's not
    Angry these days, she cries also.
    We've tried to cheer things up, although
Our mother stays in bed a lot.

Father sits with us here and reads
Tales about heroes' noble deeds.
    Once we'd have asked for nothing more
    When things at home got lonely, for
Father sits with us here and reads.

Our Uncle Fuehrer's here all day.
He can't talk much, of course, or play;
    He's driving enemies from our land.
    Safe near to him, we're lucky and
Our Uncle Fuehrer's here all day.

We know they're doing this for us;
They said so. If you make a fuss,
    The whole thing's worse for everyone;
    We just wish that they'd get it done;
We know they're doing this for us.

We'd rather sleep in our own bed
And our room, just the same. We're fed;
    We're warm enough. Still, it feels strange —
    Like it all suddenly could change;
We'd rather sleep in our own bed.

DR. JOSEPH GOEBBELS
MINISTER FOR PROPAGANDA

—23 April 1945.

*(Besides nursery rhymes and sources already
cited, he quotes his own early literary efforts.)*

I play, here, for my family
The role I've played for Germany:
Reading preposterous folk tales
To children till pure faith prevails
Over the facts. Or else I read
Carlyle and *The Nibelungenlied*
To the Chief — he could give up hope
Too soon.

Brave king, wait yet a little while...

I chart his horoscope,
Cite doctrines, miracles or quote
The texts we Jesuits get by rote —

*Dear God, make me pure and nice
So I'll get to Paradise. —*

Whatever lies keep him alive
Until the Russian tanks arrive.
The rest beg him to escape, fly
South. No; Berlin's the place to die.
Here we can say he perished with
His front-line fighters. Then our myth
Takes root, our *Goetterdaemmerung*
Lies waiting to be told and sung,
Once more casting its spell over the young.

So let the vulgar mobs curse and abominate Hitler.

Like Alaric, we'll disappear.
Only the man defeated here,
Betrayed and trampled down in scorn,
Can lay low till that time's reborn
When he can rise to reign in glory.
Then, we become *their* fairy story.

The day will come when all will go to pieces;
The mob will snarl and roar, "Crucify him!"

We whose lives, whose writings came
To nothing — we'll script their lives' aim.
We failures are the texts they'll read,
Nay-sayers who'll become their creed.
I, who can't help but see how hollow
That Fuehrer is I can't help follow,
Create in him the eucharist they'll all swallow.

Then shall we stand unshakeable and sing, "Hosannah!"

They're lickerish for this world now. All
You set your tongue to turns to gall.
Sick of their own taste, sick of winning,
They'll think of us. That's a beginning.

VI

24 – 27 APRIL 1945
LOYALTIES

CHORUS: OLD LADY BARKEEP

Old Lady Barkeep says we should
Live for our Folk, the common good,
Family virtues and motherhood,
    As bees live for their comb.
    But if you're stuck in Rome,
You screw whoever Romans screw;
Principally, those who depend on you;
Old Lady Barkeep always knew
    Betrayal begins at home.

ALBERT SPEER
ARMAMENTS MINISTER

—24 April 1945.

(Koniev's infantry from the South and Zhukov's from the North and East are nearing the city center. Having confessed disobedience, Speer bid Hitler a last farewell. Pausing in the ruined Chancellery he had built for Hitler, he recalls lines from Faust.*)*

His voice
cold as his
handshake. Not
even a kind word
for my family.

The gallery 480 feet long; twice
the Hall of Mirrors at Versailles.

The Thousand Year Reich!

Charred timber; armchairs
scattered; table legs sticking
through the rubble; a broken wheel;
beer; half-eaten sandwiches...

Galileo: Nature cannot grow an animal
beyond a certain size. It falls apart
of its own weight; turns clumsy, monstrous....

The Theory of Ruin Value! We
didn't even make good wreckage!

My father: "You have all said
goodbye to your senses."

Still
I was the
Largest boy in
School, which spared
Me from many a thrashing.

My professor: "Do you think you have
created something? It's showy; that's all."

Still
With what
Joy we gave
Ourselves to these
Designs, to the headlong
Months of drawing, matching
Materials. In eleven months we
Built this. That was Impossible. We
Had two days left over.

4500 workers in two shifts
2300 more throughout the Reich

We did
Things men
Cannot, things
We could not do. We
Knew no limit. Factories
Were running, the Reichsmark
Sound. We won our lands back; we
Could lift our heads again in Europe.

Still
I feel it,
Still above my
Shoulders like a
Host of angels, that
Ghostly providence we had
Imagined, that benison....

Exalted Spirit, you gave me, gave me everything
For which I asked.

> The skylight broken in,
> the great chandelier
> its lusters crackling underfoot.
> That brilliance extinguished.

Nov. 10: Krystal Nacht. Glass of
Jewish shop-fronts in the public streets.

> Then
> Should I
> Go on building
> Nothing? Even my
> Father, could even he
> Resist the temptation to
> Build so much? At Nuremberg,
> My Cathedral of Ice, with pillars
> Formed by searchlights...

Am I a god? I feel so light!

> Visible to 25,000 feet where
> they merge to a general glow.

July 1: The execution of Ernst Roehm.
March 5: The "Commissar Decree."

> Yes, we did
> what humans could not. Must
> not. We passed
> all limit.

And Goethe notes: "It is provided for
that trees do not vault into the Heavens."

> Now the searchlights sweep right, sweep left.
> In such a Spring, the thin ice in the mind....

                    dark skaters
              glide across the clear
           face of the abyss.

        ...won't hold up any longer.

    𝕬𝖊 𝖈𝖆𝖗𝖗𝖞 𝖙𝖍𝖊 𝖗𝖚𝖇𝖇𝖑𝖊
    𝕬𝖈𝖗𝖔𝖘𝖘 𝖙𝖔 𝕹𝖔𝖙𝖍𝖎𝖓𝖌𝖓𝖊𝖘𝖘.

                                    Provinces revolt,
              the cells turn traitorous, each building its own
        way past all limit or design. Treachery becomes
              a mode of life. We call it freedom.

                Suicide. One more
              betrayal. Some will go
                 to firing squads; some to
                      prison like a
                cancer ward or a
                      cocoon.

        The healthy organism grows, not in
        accordance with its past, what has
        been done to it, but with the future,
        what it should become.

           No more cathedrals, no reception halls.

              Sometimes, I would leave my parents' formal
              parlor with its glittering chandeliers,
              its sham fireplace, and slip down to
              play with the porter's daughter, Frieda.
              The spare, simple quarters of a crowded,
              close-knit family...

        Tin shacks to get this week's survivors
        through next winter.

              How will my wife, my unshaken
              wife, survive? I have seen too little
                 of my children...

MAGDA GOEBBELS

— 24 April 1945.

(Magda reflects on her shifting allegiances.)

i

No one would dare stay constant to
The sort who've kept good faith with me.
      They hang on, need to lean on you;
No one would dare stay constant to
      Weaklings. With *your* life to squeak through,
      What use could some such milksops be?
No one would dare stay constant to
The sort who've kept good faith with me.

ii

Who should you turn allegiance to?
The strong dare treat you faithlessly,
      Hack through those bonds that hamper you.
Who should you turn allegiance to?
      They don't look back at what they do;
      Trampling down all bounds, they go free.
Who should you turn allegiance to?
The strong dare treat you faithlessly.

iii

Raise your child up devotedly;
Once grown, he goes off his own way.
　　　How trivial you must seem to be.
Raise your child up devotedly
　　　And he thinks that you need him; he
　　　Sees no real reason not to stray.
Raise your child up devotedly;
Once grown, he goes off his own way.

iv

Then what's your true course? Turn away;
Look strong; they can't help but stay true.
　　　You've learned what wage loyalties pay.
Then what's your true course? Turn away
　　　So that they'll need you; so they'll stay
　　　Too scared to dare break ties with you.
Then what's your true course? Turn away;
Look strong; they can't help but stay true.

THE GOEBBELS CHILDREN

—24 April 1945.

*(The children appeared unaware they would
be sacrificed in a display of loyalty to Hitler.)*

Our father came here. We came with our mother.
We play games and sing songs; still, we're not happy.
Whatever they say, we tell them we believe.
Of course they feed us, dress us, say they care
About us, love us. How long would our lives
Last if they knew we know that that's a lie?

We know our father's business is to lie
To others, to the radio, to our mother;
Their work is to believe or lose their lives.
Our work, too. Since we're fed and warm, we're happy
To tell our father anything he'd care
To hear. We know he, too, wants to believe.

Our father reads to us now — make-believe
Tales where the hero's struck down and will lie
There past help; then some princess comes to care
About him. This will cure him like a mother.
In the end, he'll rise up and they'll be happy
Evermore. This will last them all their lives

As no real thing lasts, not even our lives.
Since we will die too, someday, we believe
Whatever makes the world seem less unhappy.
We dream up wilder tales, believe worse lies,
Say things we know can't happen; then our mother
Won't know what we suppose. That way, she'll care

For us, not as we'd like to have her care
But at least then she'll let us keep our lives.
We must find more ways to persuade our mother
We still believe she loves us, still believe
She's strong and certain, though we know she'll lie
With anyone she thinks could make her happy

Even a little. We might have been happy
Even a little, too, if *they* could care
For us but hate each other. So we lie,
Since all around us people lose their lives
With no food, no love, nothing to believe.
Knowing that, we draw closer to our mother.

We tell our mother her love makes us happy
Since we believe nobody else could care
So much. And life goes on: she needs that lie.

EVA BRAUN

—25 April 1945.

(Berlin is encircled. Eva picks her album's fi-
nal snapshots. Besides American songs, she
sings a German song popularized by Zarah
Leander.)

Here's EVA WITH HITLER'S SECRETARIES. They
All loved Him. He wanted them, each one,
Married inside His staff. Then they would stay
And work for Him. That's lovely Daran;
She married General Christian. *Who might this be?*
Hans, Traudl's husband — killed, though, later on.

Fuer Liebe? Fuer Liebe? Jawohl!

ADOLF TRAINING BLONDI — she was able
To sit up or roll over and play dead.
But books quote him: "It's far more worth your trouble
To train a woman." Don't buy all you've read;
He never dared bring Blondi to the table.
Why not? Eva's rules; He did what she said.

When your heart's on fire,
You must realize...

ADOLF WITH DR. GOEBBELS — impatient,
Waiting to hear how France and England
Were planning to respond to His invasion
Of Poland. *The beginning of the end!*
I wouldn't say that. You know that our nation
Needed space and we lost almost no men.

Smoke gets in your eyes.

LEAVING THE BERGHOF. *He walked with a cane?*
As time went by. *When did you last go there?*
We had no time to go back up again,
Not after Stalingrad. Everywhere
Things went all wrong. *And all these tall young men...?*
Most of them had been killed within the year.

When a lovely flame dies...

EVA WITH HER SISTER ILSE. *So you two*
Stayed in close touch? Ever since we'd been kids.
But Ilse, then, called Him a demon who
Would drag us and our Folk to the abyss.
So? We had to part. *Why? Wasn't that true?*
But that's so cruel; how could she say it?

For Love, then? For Love, then?
Yes, sir! Jawohl!

DR. JOSEPH GOEBBELS
MINISTER FOR PROPAGANDA

—26 April 1945.

(Soviet spearheads link up northwest of Ber-
lin. Bits of nursery rhymes amd The Nibe-
lungenlied *run through Goebbels' thoughts.)*

Want to go to my attic;
Want to get my kindling;
There stands a little hunchback man
Who keeps my woodpile dwindling.

Rats find time, in a sinking boat,
To sink teeth in each other's throat.
Today, Bormann and I were able
To so twist and distort the cable
Goering sent from our Southern Headquarters
(Following precisely the Chief's orders!)
That the Chief, incensed, had the swine
Deposed, disgraced, forced to resign.
Bormann, now, finding pork's in season,
Has that swine penned up for high treason!

Want to go to my chamber now;
Want to say my prayer;
There stands a little hunchback man
Who starts in laughing there.

The Reds drive closer every minute;
I can't last out the week; what's in it
For me to lance that pusbag? Please —
Real traitors don't just grow on trees.
You take what's there and do your best.
If treachery did not exist,
Mankind would just have to create it.
Where there's no Judas, cursed and hated,
No God stands to be consecrated....

Then while the high lord Sigfrid
                          bent down to the brook and drank,
Hagen stabbed straight through the cross;
                          so from the wound there sprang
The hero's heart's blood, spilling
                          out over Hagen's clothes.
No warrior, now or ever, so falsely carried out his oaths.

With no stab in the back, what could
Authenticate the hero's blood?
That lamb we sacrificed today,
Given the time, would find some way
To cut *our* throats. We Nazis used to say
The Future's never been in doubt;
The Past's what we must still work out.

Want to go to my bench, now;
Want to try to pray;
There stands a little hunchback man
Who seems about to say:

I build that Past others will use
When they need some lie or excuse
To do exactly what they choose.

My dearest child, I beg of you,
Pray for the little hunchback, too.

MARTIN BORMANN
PERSONAL SECRETARY TO THE FUEHRER

—26 April 1945.

*(Bormann and Goebbels joined to convince
Hitler that Goering had tried to usurp his
powers.)*

My Beautiful Momsy,
    You made me and my life rich...richer than Rockefeller and
Morgan and all the millionaires at once.

> Mine! Got him! Right between
> The fucking antlers. That stuffed fat
>   Head, stuck up on my wall!

I'm so glad we got...we've had all nine children.

> I really had to hump it this time.
> Goering's shrewd, that one. His cable
>   Looked innocent, all right.

Me alone, I can't love you enough.

> Goebbels got in on it, too —
> Getting the Chief to see that as
>   A fast grab for his offices.

All ten have got to join in to respond right.

> We had him screaming, "Treason! Treachery!"
> Forgetting he said, two days ago,
>   "Let Goering negotiate."

Give my love to...no...give my *regards* to "M".

> Screwed him. Stamped as a traitor.
> Lost all offices. Out of the Party.
>   Still, he *could* "explain."

She's way inferior to you but I'm still glad my will and passion overcame
her.

> The trick: a cable in the Chief's name
> Ordering his immediate execution —
> Before the Chief gets wind.

Well, I *have* been a horrible, wild ruffian.

> Who's left now? Goebbels. Speer.
> Both competent but they're no problem.
> Himmler. Only Himmler.

Too bad she never had no...never had a baby by me. You could help her
raise it right.

> Got them every one. Like a fly tape.
> They all sprawl there on their backs
> Stuck in the gold slime.

When can I retire, dearest Moms, and devote my life to my family, my
library, and the prudent lives of cabbages and cabbage butterflies?

> Their legs twitching in the sunlight
> Like girls getting fucked. They hum;
> They buzz some till they die.

Still, in all our tribulations, we got one consolation:
> Who is our first and our last?
> Who is our sacred treasure?
> Who is our everything best?
> Who is our gladsome pleasure?
Daddy and all nine children: Our Mommy!

> Ever thine,

> M.

> (M. for Martin. "M" for Manya.
> My actress. My mistress. Let that
> Gnaw at her a little.)

HEINRICH•HIMMLER
REICHSFUEHRER•SS

•26•APRIL•1945•

(As Himmler shaved each morning, his adjutant, Brandt, read him the day's reports. MM = 82.)

```
ADJUTANTS•MUST•ASK•PERMISSION•
BEFORE•DELIVERING•SUCH•REPORTS
CUTS•OF•THIS•SORT•CAN•BE•VERY•
DANGEROUS•SUBJECT•TO•INFECTION
ESPECIALLY•NEAR•THE•THROAT•THE

FUEHRER•TRAPPED•INSIDE•BERLIN•
GOOD•THING•I•DIDN'T•REPORT•TO•
HIM•THERE•AS•HE•COMMANDED•BUT•
INSTEAD•SENT•GEBHART•THE•AMIS•
JOINED•UP•WITH•THE•SOVIETS•WHO

KNOWS•WHEN•THEY•WILL•BEGIN•TO•
LIQUIDATE•EACH•OTHER•THEN•EACH
MAY•BID•FOR•OUR•HELP•IS•THERE•
NO•NEWS•NOT•SO•UTTERLY•OMINOUS
ONLY•THIS•A•M•SEVERAL•AMERICAN

PLANES•BOMBED•HITLERS•BERGHOF•
QUITE•GHASTLY•WAIT•GOERING•THE
REICHSMARSCHALL•CUT•OUT•OF•THE
SUCCESSION•DISOWNED•DECLARED•A
TRAITOR•&•IF•NOT•EXECUTED•HES•

UNDER•ARREST•WHY•THATS•A•MAJOR
VICTORY•RIGHT•THERE•I•MAY•YET•
WIN•OUT•&•TAKE•POWER•THAT•LETS
YOU•FACE•THE•DAY•WITH•A•LITTLE
ZEST•AND•FAITH•IN•MANS•FUTURE•
```

AFTER ALL HITLER SURROUNDED IN
BERLIN & GOERING CANT SUCCEED
CAN THIS MEAN ANYONE BUT ME TO
DIRECT THE STATE YET HOWD THIS
EVER HAPPEN BORMANN MUST HAVE

FOUND OUT ABOUT SOME OVERTURE
GOERING HAD MADE TO EISENHOWER
HEAVEN PRESERVE US IF HE KNEW
ID MET SOMEONE FROM THE WORLD
JEWISH CONGRESS OR IF ANYBODY

KNEW ID SEEN COUNT BERNADOTTE
LAST WEEK TO HOLD NEGOTIATIONS
MY GOD THEYD HAVE MY NECK IN A
NOOSE BEFORE YOU COULD SAY BOO
OR WORST OF ALL IF HE KNEW MY

PART IN THE ASSASSINATION PLOT
QUIT WORRYING ABOUT THAT WEVE
RETRACED & COVERED OUR TRACKS
SCRUPULOUSLY WE "DISINFECTED"
THOSE THAT COULD MAKE OUR LIFE

UNCOMFY WEVE GOT PLENTY ON THE
VERY FEW LEFT THAT COULD TALK
WORRYS SO BAD FOR YOUR HEALTH
YOU CAN PUT A MATCH TO FAT SIR
ZEPPELIN WHEN YOU CHOOSE RELAX

FORMER REICHSMARSCHALL
HERMANN GOERING

—26 April 1945.

(At the Obersalzberg, under house arrest by SS troops, Goering imagines himself interrogated.)

Good day, Herr Goering. Just relax;
We represent an organization
You yourself founded and designed:
Gestapo. We know you wouldn't mind
A brief, informal conversation
To help establish a few facts —

Now: General von Blomberg, once
Our Defense Minister...? *Dropped from staff*
For marrying a prostitute.
Perhaps not quite; her ill-repute
Came down to one nude photograph.
Who'd told Blomberg she'd been cleared? Not you?

Then General Fritsch, once our admired
Commander-in-Chief? *Exonerated:*
Though he'd been charged with sodomy.
False charges? *Mistaken identity.*
When was the general reinstated?
By whom was the false witness hired?

Again, Ernst Roehm, the onetime head
Of Hitler's SA, the Brown Shirts?
He was my friend. Yet, with a spot,
Thus, someone damned him. The SS shot
Him in his cell. No doubt this hurts,
But just what was it his "friend" said?

We know you've sought a soldier's honor
And lived only for your good name.
Dear Reichsmarschall, though, you seem nervous...?
You know these were all acts of service
To my land, my Leader.... And to your shame?
If I'd done less.... You'd be a goner?

Well...

[takes out Hitler's cable]

    FOR PAST SERVICES TO THE NATION
WE SPARE YOU THE DEATH PENALTY.
You gave your honor for his sake
Then, step by step, you let him take
Your self-respect, your loyalty
Down to this last humiliation:

Labelled a traitor, stripped and guarded.
I kept true faith with him alone.
I admit, sometimes, being loyal
To him meant other men's betrayal.
Still, by that loyalty a man's shown....
That man justly should be rewarded?

You said, as Prussia's police czar,
"Each police bullet...*is my own bullet.*"

[takes a bullet from his pocket]

You taught us agents Nazi rigor:
"Shoot high; shoot wide...

[Goering and his interrogator together]

                        but pull the trigger."

[inserts the bullet in a revolver]

Here's one for you, sir; why not pull it?

[salutes and leaves]

Thanks.

[hurls the revolver at the door]

Logic doesn't go that far.

DR. JOSEPH GOEBBELS
MINISTER FOR PROPAGANDA

—27 April 1945.

*(The previous evening, Hitler held a farewell
ceremony. Besides sources already cited,
Goebbels quotes bits of* Don Giovanni.*)*

The girls that haunt our movie screen
Ghosted my nights. Each played her scene
Then passed, indifferent, to the next —
One take more from a used-up text.

> *Girls are mighty dear now —*
> *You know what I mean:*
> *Pennypiece will get you five;*
> *Thruppence for fifteen.*

And what have I been but His ghost,
Ersatz or stand-in at the most?
If slim shapes shuddered in my embrace,
Back of my eyes they saw His face.
Behind *their* eyes, just out of sight,
What face, like Helen's, ruled my night?

There lived a right royal maiden   far off in Burgundy;
Through all the lands and nations   none lovelier than she.
Kriemhilda was she called there;   she shone in beauty bright
That when, full grown, a woman,   brought death to many a noble knight.

You drive your sting deep in each one;
Get up and it's your own blood gone.
Your pulse, each time, throbs stronger, taller;
Each one you rise from leaves you smaller
And how much stature can you add
By counting up the holes you've had?

155

Ma in Ispaña, son già mille e tre.

Magda: she's that black hole in space
Nature abhors, men can't help chase,
But only fools rush in to fill.
We drained each other's juices till
Nothing was left but the dry bone.
Knowing how shrill our thirsts had grown,
He banned all sustenance but His own
And, emptiest, wolf-thin, vacuous,
Sucked the last marrow out of us.

𝕾𝖍𝖊 𝖘𝖕𝖔𝖐𝖊: 𝖎𝖓 𝖋𝖎𝖓𝖊 𝖙𝖍𝖗𝖊𝖆𝖉, 𝖘𝖎𝖑𝖐𝖊𝖓,　　𝕴'𝖑𝖑 𝖘𝖊𝖜 𝖜𝖎𝖙𝖍 𝖘𝖊𝖈𝖗𝖊𝖙 𝖈𝖆𝖗𝖊
𝕬 𝖘𝖒𝖆𝖑𝖑 𝖈𝖗𝖔𝖘𝖘 𝖔𝖓 𝖍𝖎𝖘 𝖌𝖆𝖗𝖒𝖊𝖓𝖙 —　　𝖜𝖆𝖗𝖗𝖎𝖔𝖗 𝖐𝖓𝖎𝖌𝖍𝖙, 𝖗𝖎𝖌𝖍𝖙 𝖙𝖍𝖊𝖗𝖊
𝖄𝖔𝖚 𝖒𝖚𝖘𝖙 "𝖕𝖗𝖔𝖙𝖊𝖈𝖙" 𝖒𝖞 𝖍𝖚𝖘𝖇𝖆𝖓𝖉.

Last night, his ceremonial
Farewell. We lined the hall.
When he reached Magda's side, he took
His gold party badge, fixed its hook
To her left breast and kissed her cheek.
She sobbed. I felt both knees go weak
As great Brunhilda, pierced one night
By the wrong bridegroom and bled white.

Che gelo è questo mai!

So I who played false all my life
Stand fast by my false god and wife,
By two whose perfidy exceeds
My own, by two whose ravening needs
Spent mine. Now no hope's left, I must
Smile: his saint of abiding trust,
So Nothing, once more, can rise from our dust.

Boys are mighty dear now —
You know what I mean:

They claim he fathered my dull son.
Madness and retardation run
In Hitler's family, not in mine.
Right here we'll staunch one soiled bloodline.

Fifteen for a feather duster;
Thruppence for sixteen.

My stone commander climbs the stairs
To take my hand. I'll take theirs.

MAGDA GOEBBELS

—27 April 1945.

I wear His badge, here, on my breast today;
    All those lost years, He must have wanted me.
I've borne old sacrifices; I obey.
    I stand restored: His heir, His deputy.

In this delirium of treachery
    On all sides, when our gods have turned away,
After the times He's scorned my company,
    I wear His badge, here, on my breast today.

Others have had His time, His gifts — but they,
    When He called on them, failed Him wretchedly.
No Knights' Cross shines like this pin I display.
    All those lost years, He must have wanted me.

He made Paulus Field Marshal, yet still he
    Surrendered Stalingrad — we thought they'd stay
Till each last man died for Him gloriously.
    I've borne old sacrifices; I obey.

Paulus! We should have known that he'd betray
    And give his men up to captivity.
No false pity will make me flinch that way.
    I stand restored: His heir, His deputy,

Though I'm their keeper, too. I can't help see
    Their eyes wavering toward me while they play.
I break down sometimes, still. How can this be
    The breast that fed them once? And yet today
        I wear His badge.

VII

28 – 30 APRIL 1945

ORGY

———————————————————————

CHORUS: OLD LADY BARKEEP

Old Lady Barkeep's bacchanal,
Beasts' brawl and orgy proved that all
Who find they face a blank stone wall
    Can still make one last stand
Against themselves. You've got to die
But, though you can't pick when or why,
You can make sure you perish by
    Nobody else's hand.
    You stay in command.

ADOLF HITLER

—28 April 1945.

(Red troops, sometimes bypassing strong points
via subway tunnels, are closing in, house to
house. Meantime, word has come that Musso-
lini has been killed by partisans.)

[takes the radio dispatch]

Benito, pattern, partner, my brother in this war,
Hung, strung by the heels above the public market.

> My brother, Edmund, hauled out
> Howling, one year after me.

One more tightrope stunt. By our clenched teeth
To twist and dangle over the gaping masses.

Spat on, defiled by his own followers. The bungler
Betrayed me always. So punished; so absolved.

> These carnivores, corpse-tearers at their vile
> Communion. What dead flesh reeking on their breath?

The wild boar bled out. Hacked apart and shared out
To the hankering mob; his flesh that died for me.

> Cast that in silver? An amulet for them
> To finger, hanging from their throats?

> Alois, my half-brother, flaunting
> My father's name: "the favorite."

Me they have called merciless who twice
Saved him from his follies; merciless
Who drew back, withheld the death stroke
At Dunkirk, Leningrad, at Moscow.

"I hoped for the great handshake of brothers."

But Edmund died the year I was eleven.

Merciless!? I devour no flesh. These vermin want...

[takes Goering's cable]

Goering: that fat mouth forever howling want:
"...that I should take control over the nation
including full powers for negotiation..."
For negotiation? Powers? After my death?

"This time no negotiations, no surrender."

[takes a Reuters dispatch]

Himmler: that viper's slack jaw, hungering for
a friend's heart, for the forbidden blood:
"...had twice contacted Count Bernadotte
arranging for capitulation of his forces..."

"Capitulation to another's will? Never!"

[takes Heinrici's memorandum]

These toothless generals wheedling their wants:
"...that our old, sick and wounded, our refugees
take shelter inside the subway tunnels where
Red shock troops are infiltrating, block by block..."
Am I not old? Not sick? This not a tunnel?

And still these vermin want...

If our Leader knew what we suffer...

Want. They, for their own lives, would not drown me?
Strangle me with own navelcord? Flush me out

If only our Leader is saved...

Like an enema, like douching after sex? Only
This flesh they want. This flesh forbidden them.

[takes up his own "Scorched Earth" directive]

"Second Fuehrer Directive, 19 March 1945:
...no human beings, no livestock, not one bag of grain,
no remaining railroad track, no house or barn left standing,
no mine still fit to work, no single well unpoisoned...."

"I want only one thing: the end! the end!"

That order: already given.

The Jews in Warsaw's tunnels. Drowned.

Blast out the river gates.
Flood out the tunnels. Now.

MARTIN BORMANN
PERSONAL SECRETARY TO THE FUEHRER

—28 April 1945.

(With Red troops a mile away, Bormann composes a last letter to his wife.)

My Precious One and Only,

  The Reds close in hourly. Treachery, desertion on every side. Even Himmler — "the faithful Heinrich!"

    Mine. One more in the bag. They don't
    Dare twitch till I tell them: Twitch.
      Brandt. Goering. Himmler.

I've seen too much ineptitude, slander, nauseating false flattery, toadying, idiocy, vanity, greed, etc., etc.

    So now we kiss off "Onkle Heinrich" —
    Just Speer and Goebbels left. As for
      Goebbels — he'll kill himself.

No wonder I'm sick of politics. Sometimes it seems only you and me stand faithful.

    And Comrade Speer botched it up, trying
    To save the whole thing for himself.
      No real enemy left.

We just think about one thing: how to serve our Chief.

    The whole Reich slips into my hands
    Since I control the Chief. Yeah, but now
      The Chief will have to bow out.

You dear, stupid...no...silly Momsy — getting jealous of a girl like "M"!
She thinks only about her friends and family.

> Who's strong enough still to save us
> A few acres in negotiations? Weak
>   Enough, though, to be some use?

You'll raise the children right, by good Nazi principles.

> The Admiral: dull, dumb Doenitz.
> The Party's tool. A friend. He'd hear
>   Sound practical advice.

Never forget to warn the children:
1. Don't play with fire or matches.
2. Don't jump in the water when you're hot.

> The trick: transfer all power to Doenitz
> But we handpick his cabinet. Myself,
>   Probably, as Party Minister.

3. If somebody offers candy to go with them, just always scream.
4. By no means always tell the truth — unless you've got to.

> The trick: suggest this to the Chief.
> The trick: convince the Chief to think he
>   Suggested it to us first.

And keep a close eye on young Eicke. She'll be meeting our soldiers; you
know where that can lead!

> Then lay back under the Chief's
> Shadow, where the live wires cross,
>   The phones, cables, radio —

Final victory must be ours — or, like you said, the order of the universe
would be all loused-up.

> Keep his voice humming on the lines,
> Feel out what forces tremble in the network,
>   Till that last, worst moment when....

If, like the old Niebelungs, we are doomed, we shall go to our deaths proudly, with heads held high.

> We got to come up under the lights,
> The guns, and scurry across the clearing
> To some more durable obscurity.

Keep well and strong, Mommy mine. Know that I am wholly and totally

Thine alone,

M.

HEINRICH • HIMMLER
FORMER • REICHSFUEHRER • SS

• 29 • APRIL • 1945 •

(His negotiations for surrender exposed,
Himmler has been declared a traitor and ex-
pelled from the party by Hitler. MM=80.)

```
A • WISE • MAN • ALWAYS • KNOWS • HE • MAY
BE • MISUNDERSTOOD • REVILED • TO • BE
CALLED • A • TRAITOR • WHEN • I • MERELY
DID • MY • BEST • TO • SAVE • OUR • TROOPS
EVEN • SAVE • HIS • OWN • LIFE • WITH • MY

FOREIGN • CONTACTS • ALSO • USING • MY
GOOD • NAME • AFTER • LONG • YEARS • OF •
HONORABLE • SERVICE • & • HARDSHIPS •
I • BORE • FOR • HIM • GETTING • RID • OF •
JEWS • GYPSIES • YOUD • THINK • I • LIKE

KILLING • ALL • THOSE • PEOPLE • O • ITS
LITTLE • THANKS • YOU • GET • BESIDES •
MY • STOMACH • CRAMPS • THERES • JUST •
NO • JUSTICE • TRUE • I • DIDNT • DO • IT •
ORIGINALLY • ONLY • FOR • IDEALISTIC

PURPOSES • I • COULD • HAVE • MADE • IT •
QUITE • IDEALISTIC • LATER • ON • AND •
REALLY • NOW • TO • KILL • THAT • MANY • &
STAY • DECENT • UPRIGHT • IDEALISTIC
THAT • DESERVES • SOMETHING • I • GAVE

UP • MY • HAPPY • CHICKEN • FARM • & • THE
VICIOUS • THINGS • THEY • CALLED • ME •
WHY • I • FAINT • JUST • SEEING • BLOOD •
YET • HARD • AS • IT • IS • WE • MUST • KEEP
ZEAL • MORALITY • & • SELF - SACRIFICE
```

DR. JOSEPH GOEBBELS
MINISTER FOR PROPAGANDA

—29 April 1945.

*(He hums nursery rhymes while considering
Himmler's defection.)*

One more laugh: now we don't need one,
We get our traitor — a guaranteed one:
Himmler, the Faithful Heinrich, caught
Worming up to Count Bernadotte,
Bargaining off his prisoners, Jews,
His camps and troops. He knows we'll lose,
And thinks they'll let him turn his coat.
Now *both* sides itch to slit his throat.

> *Oh, what do we geese wear for clothes?*
> *Gi, ga, gock!*
> *We march out barefoot, day and night,*
> *Dressed in featherwear of white,*
> *Gi, ga, gock!*
> *We've only got one smock!*

While strong men scramble to betray
All they once killed for, guess who'll stay
True to the end? — the poor and weak,
Dumb beasts or children, the Lord's meek
Like Eva Braun or Bormann's wife
Who can't quickchange to match this life;
Stuck with one story — their own past
Loves or beliefs — they'll stand steadfast.

> *What do we geese eat for food?*
> *Gi, ga, gack!*
> *Summertimes we pick the meadow;*
> *Winters, farm wives keep us fed, oh,*
> *Gi, ga, gack!*
> *Out of the oatmeal sack!*

The Reds won't spare me a new cloak.
So me, I keep faith — what a joke!
Now he forbids me any role
In his death scene. What can control
And keep men true to you forever?
It's just the same as children: never
Show loyalty to them, then they
Stick tight — you can't drive them away.

> *How do geese spend Martin's Mass?*
> *Gi, ga, geck!*
> *Our Leader brings us from our pen*
> *To Martin's schmaltzy feast and then,*
> *Gi, ga, geck!*
> *It seems they wring our neck!*

As for my daughters, they behave.
They must imagine they can save
Their lives by doing what they should.
Well, once upon a time, you could.
But Helga knows; the oldest one
Who took the place of my dull son
Lapped up my words like her life's blood.
Too bad: you die, now, *if* you're good.

HELGA GOEBBELS

—29 April 1945.

(Goebbels' oldest child was 12. Partly to make up for not being the boy he wanted, she became an ardent Nazi. As the fighting neared, Blondi was killed to test the cyanide capsules, then the puppies were destroyed.)

What if your dog got hit by a car?
A daughter comes; it's hard to care
It's right: you've got to kill the thing.
If she'll be bright or what she'll think.
When Fafner, my dachshund, got run down,
Still, Father taught me — like a son;
Father shot him. It was his duty.
My Mother's got to admit I'm pretty.

Blondi's litter got killed today.
I mind the little ones; I obey.
Helmut's a boy; they've got to be brave.
I learned the ways we ought to behave.
He bawled and bawled that it's not fair.
I have blue eyes; I have blonde hair.
I smacked his face. That was all wrong.
I liked all the right books and songs.

They'd not get fed or cared for here;
I stayed to hear our Uncle Fuehrer
Strangers would just chase them away.
When the rest skipped out to play.
Our Fuehrer, history's greatest man,
Father's sister might take them in
Shows how true faith and steadfastness
Only they'd make her house a mess.

Hardens us for harsh tasks. He teaches
Blondi snarled: no one could touch
Those hurt past all help need a hand
Her young. She didn't understand.
To end their pain. Nobody would
I tried; I wanted to be good.
Want life where there's no faith, no love.
Father, forgive me. Let me live.

GENERAL HERMANN FEGELEIN
SS ADJUTANT TO THE BUNKER

—29 April 1945, 0200 hours.

(On April 28, Gretl Braun's husband, about to flee Berlin with an actress, was arrested. After Himmler's defection, Fegelein — his aide — was questioned, then led out and shot. Meantime, a general orgy had begun in the Bunker.)

[sweet jesus bleeding asshole no they cant
just shoot me like this   can they
my own men]
               in the guards station
singing   against regulations
whats worse smoking
               [and with no trial
my own brotherinlaw   shit then
my wifes sisters husband   shit
then lover]
          common soldiers
puking in the passage where the chief
takes meals
          [I had this sick world
by the short hair   an ss general
at only 37   blue eyes   blond
superior physique]
              broke into the
medical supplies or else the officers
good wine
          [first run on any snatch
down here   my stupid wife to put in
a good word to the chief]
             the bad phonograph
"Red Roses for Remembrance"

                    [I had carlotta
good as anything of goebbels   and enough
swiss coin pinched out so I could
buy in on the best lake there]
                         screwing her
while theyre dancing in the same room
that isnt done
                [shit once hes good
and dead shit whod know me
retired and respectable]
                    radio girl
spreadeagled with her pants off
                         [by now evas
heard about carlotta but she ought to care
about her little sister   say she put
a good word to   no]
                    I could have
had her any time I said
                    [say this
was a test at the last minute
the reprieve   no]
                another gun squad
in off of whore patrol   thats no bad
piece theyve got there
                    [say I ordered
them to save me   no]
                    shit better ankles
on a cart horse
                [say martin   reichsleiter
bormann   my best buddy   say he could
put in   no]
                    staring at me like
some numbskull serb
                    [martin said I was in
on himmlers sellout to the west   I just
wish to sweet shit Id have known]
                         but I
screwed them every one
                    [theyll leave me
where   and come back to these cunts
who even knows their names]

174

no   not
that one in the dentists chair
                    [after
I sold him   my own boss   to martin
martin   his word fixed my ass]
                              ivan
will burn you out like pissants
                    [after
my loyal service   the slovak gangs
jews   the july assassins   I
sent them to the meat hooks]
                         and thats
gods mercy to what ivans got saved up
for you
        [say Ive got this pregnant wife
no]
     so warm it up for ivan
                         [but I as good
as crucified whole regiments for him
him]
        shit youll just pray for vaseline

[sweet jesus no   they cant just
can they
          shit   shit   shit

EVA ♭ HITLER, geb. BRAUN

—30 April 1945, 1510 hours.

*(After the improvised civil marriage, Eva sits
on her bed alone. Hitler has gone to dictate
his will before their mutual deaths. Fragments
of the Mass and the Catholic wedding ser-
vice run through her mind.)*

Consummatum est.

It is accomplishèd. My mother's will
    be done.   Is done.

    How many died
so I could carry her
      His name: the Dodd girl,
     the Valkyrie, Ley's wife,
Geli. When we were kids
  we looked at the eclipse
through snapshot negatives. They held
    their longing up to Him; their sight
    flashed out.

*To thee do we cry, poor banished
children of Eve*

    I kissed His picture
through glass; the sun
     outside my windows
sneered at me. At the Munich Station,
   His train had gone; all we saw
    was tail lights. Never
     a love note; never a word
in public. He was
    never there. Twice I tried
to kill myself. Only my first

"suicide" brought Him
to me. Tonight
the third. For dead sure.

What God hath joined together
let no man put asunder.

A boy, they'd find Him
catching sunlight
in a pocket mirror, playing it
around the courtyard. Even now
He has gone off with Traudl
to dictate His will. Since He cannot
have His will.

Therefore shall a man leave father
and mother and cleave to his wife.
They shall be one flesh.

And even if He came, He
would be missing; I
could look through Him
like a worn-out lantern slide. The priest
held up the monstrance
they said held the Host;
we cast our eyes down. But I
crept up in the empty chapel,
one day, to the holy case. There
the monstrance
rayed out gleaming
like the May sun. But in the
center, the tiny glass bead,
I could see nothing.
Nothing.

And yet I have these albums, these
pictures proving it all so.
He leaves me
my crossed-out name, my
new name on a piece of paper:

Eva ⚭ Hitler, geb. Braun.
Even the wedding ceremony...
I had to wear my long black taffeta.

With this ring I thee wed;
This gold and silver I thee bring.

This ring delivered for me
by the Gestapo...

I am black but beautiful
ye daughters of Jerusalem.

...this ring torn off some Jew's hand.

in templo sancto tuo in Jerusalem.

I am the Black Bride that will be
devoured, that will pass
into Him like a film stalled,
burning through, or reeling
back into itself.
Like all the women, foreigners, all
our beautiful young men —
all small as ants under
the magnifying glass
He reads His maps by.

Consummatum est.

To be so soon consumed and
never consummated.

O Thou who hast created
all things out of nothing...

Now each one has the nothing
they fought for. My mother —
she only wants it all
to mean her meaning; something

instead of life. To tell the neighbors.
And that I give her. She
can rest.

Ite. Missa est.

My mother's will be mine.
Is mine.

It is accomplishèd.

ADOLF HITLER

—30 April 1945, 1520 hours.

(Red troops are in Voss and Wilhelm Strasse. Hitler and Eva have withdrawn to his sitting room; she has already killed herself. Besides phrases from Die Goetterdaemmerung, Lohengrin *and his favorite Disney films, he recalls his own earlier statements.)*

"To master the world and then
Destroy it."

More than fifty millions. More.
Who killed as much; who ever?

"Casualties? But that's exactly what
The young men are there for."

Russian: twenty million.
Jew: seven million, five hundred thousand.

That many and what good? What does
That save you? It still goes on, on...

Traitors on every side! Lies! Lies!

One gift, finally, to my faithful:
Last night, my secretaries, cook,
The short-wave girls — one capsule each
To save them from these Mongols'
Greasy pricks. A waste. Some
Will sneak off West; some
Wait for the Red tanks...overcome
By their own lust...

𝕯𝖊𝖈𝖊𝖎𝖛𝖊𝖉! 𝕯𝖊𝖈𝖊𝖎𝖛𝖊𝖉! 𝕾𝖍𝖆𝖒𝖊𝖑𝖊𝖘𝖘𝖑𝖞 𝕯𝖊𝖈𝖊𝖎𝖛𝖊𝖉!
𝕭𝖊𝖙𝖗𝖆𝖞𝖆𝖑! 𝕭𝖊𝖙𝖗𝖆𝖞𝖆𝖑! 𝕰𝖝𝖈𝖊𝖊𝖉𝖎𝖓𝖌 𝖆𝖑𝖑 𝖗𝖊𝖛𝖊𝖓𝖌𝖊!

Pole: three million.

"Casualties never can be high enough.
They are the seeds of future heroism."

And seven at one blow, one blow,
And seven at one blow.

Last night, again, the movie: Witzleben,
General Joke Life, hauled up, wriggling
On the meat hook, handcuffed, naked,
Six times to strangle. Sir Choke Alive.
Five times hauled down, brought back,
Couldn't even beg to die. Scrawny pizzle
Couldn't come again. Not even dust.
Couldn't...

Gypsy: four hundred...four...
four hundred thousand.

Not one truly grateful.

Shovelling lime in a latrine. Oh,
It's dragon seed. We played it three times;
No satisfaction. Not even...

I bring you not peace but a sword.
This death in honor. This seed in the earth.

French: five hundred thousand.
Jugoslav: five hundred...

[turns to Eva's body]

Not even her who understood she died
For me. Who chose. Even to come here —
A mortal impudence.

𝕿𝖍𝖊 𝕲𝖗𝖆𝖎𝖑 𝕶𝖓𝖎𝖌𝖍𝖙 𝖒𝖚𝖘𝖙 𝖓𝖊𝖛𝖊𝖗 𝖇𝖊 𝖘𝖚𝖘𝖕𝖊𝖈𝖙𝖊𝖉;
𝕺𝖓𝖈𝖊 𝖗𝖊𝖈𝖔𝖌𝖓𝖎𝖟𝖊𝖉, 𝖙𝖍𝖊𝖓 𝖒𝖚𝖘𝖙 𝖍𝖊 𝖇𝖊 𝖌𝖔𝖓𝖊.

Betrayed to! Lies! Betrayed to!

German: spineless worms. Only four...
four hundred...only four...

What use are facts, statistics?
To not need, ever, anyone alive. Whose
Death? Whose death can show you
More fit to live? Whose...

Who's afraid of the big bad wolf,
Ha-ha-ha-ha-ha!

Tell me I have to die, then. You can't be
Sure enough. My name on every calendar.
Relentless, every April, my birthdate
Comes around. My death: my lickass general.
My lackey. My Will scrubs it all out,
All of you, all gone...

"I go with the precision and
security of a sleepwalker."

I pick my time, my place. I take
This capsule tight between my teeth...
Set this steel cold against my jaw...
Clench, clench...and once more I am
Winning,
          winning,
                    winning...

MAGDA GOEBBELS

—30 April 1945.

(After Dr. Haase gave them shots of mor-
phine, Magda gave each of of her children
an ampule of potassium cyanide in a spoon.)

This is the needle that we give
Soldiers and children when they live
Near the front, in primitive
    Conditions or real dangers;
This is the spoon we use to feed
Men trapped in trouble or in need,
When weakness or bad luck might lead
    Them to the hands of strangers.

This is the room where you can sleep
Your sleep out, curled up under deep
Protective layers that will keep
    You safe till all harm's past.
This is the bed where you can rest
In perfect silence, undistressed
By noise or nightmares, as my breast
    Once held you soft but fast.

This is the Doctor who has brought
Your needle with your special shot
To hush you so you won't get caught
    Off guard or unprepared.
I am your nurse who'll comfort you;
I nursed you, fed you till you grew
Too big to feed; now you're all through
    Fretting or feeling scared.

This is the glass tube that contains
Calm that will spread down through your veins
To free you finally from all pains
    Of going on in error.

This tiny pinprick sets the germ
Inside you that fills out its term
Till you can feel yourself grow firm
    Against all doubt, all terror.

Into this spoon I break the pill
That stiffens the unsteady will
And hardens you against the chill
    Voice of a world of lies.
This amber medicine implants
Steadfastness in your blood; this grants
Immunity from greed and chance,
    And from all compromise.

This is the serum that can cure
Weak hearts; these pure, clear drops insure
You'll face what comes and can endure
    The test; you'll never falter.
This is the potion that preserves
You in a faith that never swerves;
This sets the pattern of your nerves
    Too firm for you to alter.

I set this spoon between your tight
Teeth, as I gave you your first bite;
This satisfies your appetite
    For other nourishment.
Take this on your tongue; this do
Remembering your mother who
So loved her Leader she stayed true
    When all the others went,

When every friend proved false, in the
Delirium of treachery
On every hand, when even He
    Had turned His face aside.
He shut himself in with His whore;
Then, though I screamed outside His door,
Said He'd not see me anymore.
    They both took cyanide.

Open wide, now, little bird;
I who sang you your first word
Soothe away every sound you've heard
    Except your Leader's voice.
Close your eyes, now; take your death.
Once we slapped you to take breath.
Vengeance is mine, the Lord God saith
    And cancels each last choice.

Once my first words marked out your mind;
Just as our Leader's phrases bind
All hearts to Him, building a blind
    Loyalty through the nation,
We shape you into a pure form.
Trapped, our best soldiers tricked the storm,
The Reds: though freezing, they felt warm
    Who stood fast to their station.

You needn't fear what your life meant;
You won't curse how your hours were spent;
You'll grow like your own monument
    To all things sure and good,
Fixed like a frieze in high relief
Of granite figures that our Chief
Accepts into His fixed belief,
    His true blood-brotherhood.

You'll never bite the hand that fed you,
Won't turn away from those that bred you,
Comforted your nights and led you
    Into the thought of virtue.
You won't be turned from your own bed;
Won't turn into the thing you dread;
No new betrayal lies ahead.
    Now no one else can hurt you.

VIII

1 MAY 1945

WAYS OUT

CHORUS: OLD LADY BARKEEP

Old Lady Barkeep took the notion
To start her own kind of devotion:
    Your Chief says, "Loyalty
Has never yet been mutual,
So I'll hang, starve or shoot you all
    Then you'll love none but me."
Still, you could find worse kinds of trouble —
Suppose that prick should prick your bubble;
You could wake up eye-deep in rubble
    To find you've been set free.

COL. GEN. GOTTHARD HEINRICI
FORMER COMMANDER, ARMY GROUP VISTULA

—1 May 1945.

*(On the 28th, Heinrici directly disobeyed
Hitler's orders; he was dismissed then ordered
to HQ on the 30th. To prevent his going, a
junior officer revealed how Rommel had
died.)*

For days I asked, I begged permission
To pull back and save our men.
                     Denied.
Twice I offered to resign, take a rifle
In the front line trenches.
                     Denied.
Now I have broken my oath, ordering
Manteuffel back out of encirclement.
So I, too, get orders: back to Ploen.
Rommel, I find only now, was not killed
At the front. Put to death by his own
Superiors. Superiors?
                     Denied. Commanders.
By *my* commanders. For years I've sworn
The enemy more numerous than we thought;
I overlooked how many were behind me.
Manteuffel ordered guards for me. Which I
Declined: I take my way. To Ploen? Obedience
Remains my habit. Besides, in two days more
Ploen should be in the hands of "enemies."
And I remain master of the slow retreat;
That *should* save lives.

MAGDA GOEBBELS

—1 May 1945.

(Having killed her children, Magda played solitaire and drank champagne until the time for her own death. She talks to an imaginary child.)

Face down, one by one, lay out six cards; the seventh lies
Face up. On top, then, rows of six, five, four, three,
Two, one — each time, the last must go
Face up. Like dormitory
Beds in a row,
The eyes

Looking at you. We link these cards, now, building always
Down; we call them "marriages." The black eight, there
On the red nine; red goes on black.
The one-eyed jack,
There, plays

On the queen of hearts or diamonds. Kings fill any space
Left vacant. We build these down long lines
Like families from the Almanach
De Gotha. Of course, mine's
Pure, centuries back.
The ace

Moves into this clear central space. Out there, things count
Upward in suits; these are called the "Foundation."
They stay — like bonds sealed in some bank's
Vaults — steadfast as the nation's
Heroes. Their ranks
Amount

To something. Now, three at a time, deal out your store
Of what's left. But play the "Foundation" piles
First; all these "marriages" exist
Only to swell their files.
But look: we missed
The four!

Sometimes you pass up just what you need. Since there's only
Us two, we'll bring back one dead card. There; you'll
Not scream for the police, I trust?
This way you learn the rules;
Don't sit and just
Feel lonely.

Still, do the best, or the worst, you can; it's all the same:
Everything plays out on you; you're just done.
Drink to the losses; add your score.
Then why not try just one
More glass, one more
Quick game?

MARTIN BORMANN
FORMER PERSONAL SECRETARY
TO THE FUEHRER

—1 May 1945.

*(Leading other survivors, Bormann leaves the
Bunker while composing an imaginary letter
to his wife.)*

Under the shadow of this tank. Rocks, rubble on all sides, sour smoke.
Everything in flames; lights.

> My sweetest Momsy, this very minute
> I am leading those few that stayed faithful
> In a slow and orderly retreat.

A fucking SS uniform! How could I be so stupid! Baur shot down in the
street. Now the Chief's dead, he could have flown us anywhere.

> No doubt I could flee Europe safely.
> It is our solemn duty to remain here
> Representing our ideals.

Thank God the stitching on these sleeve patches comes loose. There;
could be a business suit. So there's Eichmann's Gestapo cellar in the
Kurfurstenstrasse. The network can pick me up there.

> We must strike onward, through to Ploen;
> Must guide Doenitz forming our government.
> It's our clear and simple duty.

At least in Schleswig-Holstein we have friends. There's the Danish
monastery. But the money's all gone to South America. And how to shake
these dolts?

We must face up now to the tragic loss
Of our heroic leader. Remember his spirit,
   The great cause for which he fought...

Thank God nobody knows my face. And I could take a Jewish surname...

TRAUDL JUNGE

—1 May 1945.

(After Bormann's group has left, several of the women wait to try threading the Russian lines to safety.)

everybody left feels free
to smoke   why should you
save your breath   doors are left
wide open   no work's left to save us
from our own devices   i have taken
His dictation one last time
His last will   i still believed
He could make it all make sense   just
the same accusations excuses lies
He never wanted this war
                                    Day
after day He'd told us He should
have started this war sooner.   Left
to go our own way. Free
to choose
                    only we don't have
ways   we don't choose   given tin
helmets and men's clothing we
wait over cigarettes and coffee
for instructions   someone to lead
us through the ruined gardens

Before us lies the ruined city
Smoking — rape, butchery, plundering.
Down here, soldiers carousing, raucous
Drunken women, our officers devising
Their own ways to die. In his room,
His coat still hanging on the rack,
His dog's leash hanging empty like
A noose...
                    And we are free to...

GEN. HELMUTH "CRUSHER KARL" WEIDLING
FORMER COMMANDANT, BERLIN

—1 May 1945.

The silence staggered me. Now a shout,
A shot or two, a scream rings out.
Looting and raping — the sounds
Of peace — rise up again.

In Chuikov's office, I told him,
"Every unnecessary casualty
Is a crime." He was not deeply
Touched by my humane concern.

Shit; it took *me* by surprise; by shock.
To the south, down avenues where
Hitler's voice rang, Red sound trucks
Lay down my law: "Lay down your weapons."

My men dead or captured, my boss
Dead if he goes to headquarters. I go
To the Russians. Who,
If they can't make me talk,

Know ways to guarantee a silence.
My echo: "Lay down your weapons."
Where my voice is the loudest voice
For peace, you know you're in trouble.

HERMANN GOERING
FORMER REICHSMARSCHALL

—1 May 1945.

(Arrested by SS troops in his castle at
Mautendorf — left him by his mother's lover
— he stands naked before a full-length bed-
room mirror.)

When I speak to you, you stand to attention.
Straighten that back up. Lift up your damn head.
You'd featherbed your life out on some pension?
Fat chance of that, Fat Man! You're here to die.
You can't haul that much pork up in the sky
And if you go down and you fry instead
You'll spit like bacon. You lost your nerve
To face the life you once had; why not try
Making your exit with some style, some verve?

Disowned and disinherited? Poor baby!
We'll make a man of you, you slab of blubber.
We'll teach you where your toes are, your spine — maybe
Work you back down to fighting weight again.
Go turn in your silk robes, your diamonds, then
Give back all the paintings, cash in your rubber
Medals for the tub. From those big loose dugs
You'll get no warm milk. Join the world of men
Where pain and death live. And check in your drugs.

You might as well find out just what you've done,
Though that's not what they'll hang you for.
You took a fine officer's wife and son;
When you came to power you supplied
Facts that got your friend, Roehm, killed. Then you lied
About Blomberg and Fritsch. To start this war,
You threatened to bomb Prague; and your lies scared
Old Hacha till he gasped, fell, almost died.
Speak up to your Chief, though — you never dared.

No; one more time, you let yourself be mastered
By someone you sucked up to — who used your blind
Faith, used your worst impulses, then the bastard
Defiled your name. You bought your consequences.
Let Speer or Funk whimper and whine repentance
Merely to piss in front and crap behind
A few days more. You can't keep all *that* skin;
Keep some honor. You signed on for your sentence;
You're in so deep, there's no out left but in.

Your father lost the good name he'd once owned
By trying to fink out on his own past —
Your mother played the whore — while he'd condoned,
Ignored that for his soft life as a vassal
To Dr. Epenstein, lord of this castle —
Which he left you, where you end up at last
And you're about to end up. Own your own
Decisions; own your men. And if some asshole
Stands to face you down, you stand alone.

HEINRICH • HIMMLER
FORMER • REICHSFUEHRER • SS

• 1 • MAY • 1945 •

(Learning that Hitler's will names Doenitz as successor, Himmler ponders alternatives. MM=104.)

```
AN • EYE-PATCH • THATS • THE • ANSWER •
BESIDES • ILL • SHAVE • MY • MOUSTACHE
CUT • MY • HAIR • ALL • WRONG • THERE • MY
DISGUISE • IS • COMPLETE • ILL • WEAR •
EYEGLASSES • NOT • THIS • PINCE-NEZ •

FALL • INTO • THE • MOBS • OF • REFUGEES
GOING • WEST • IVE • BECOME • HEINRICH
HITZINGER • WITH • THE • LEGITIMATE •
IDENTITY • CARD • OF • A • SOLDIER • WE •
JUST • SHOT • AS • A • DESERTER • STILL •

KROSIG • SAYS • THE • ONLY • HONORABLE
LINE • IS • JUST • DRIVE • STRAIGHT • TO
MONTGOMERYS • H • Q • & • TELL • THEM • MY
NAME • IS • HEINRICH • HIMMLER • I • CAN
OFFER • MY • FORCES • SURRENDER • I • AM

PERSONALLY • RESPONSIBLE • WITHOUT
QUALIFICATION • FOR • ALL • S • S • ACTS
REALLY • NOW • WHY • NOT • JUST • SIMPLY
SHOOT • MYSELF • COULD • WE • GO • NORTH
TO • SCHLESWIG-HOLSTEIN • THEN • SET

UP • AN • S • S • GOVT • WE • MIGHT • OBTAIN
VERY • FAVORABLE • TERMS • FROM • THE •
WEST • SO • THEN • AT • THE • VERY • WORST
YOUD • KEEP • OUT • OF • THE • HANDS • OF •
ZHUKOV • AND • THE • RED • TROOPS • THE •
```

AMERICANS • OBVIOUSLY • THEY • WOULD
BE • BEST • BUT • WE • HAVE • NO • JEWS • WE
CAN • TRADE • NO • PRISONERS • WE • MUST
DO • WHAT • WE • CAN • TO • CONVINCE • OUR
ENEMIES • THESE • ARE • SUBSTANTIAL •

FORCES • BETTER • YET • WHY • CANT • WE •
GO • TO • FLENSBURG • WITH • DOENITZ • &
HIS • GANG • THAT • HITLERS • WILL • PUT
INTO • OFFICE • LINE • UP • OUR • CARS • &
JOIN • HIS • ENTOURAGE • WHOLL • DARE •

KEEP • US • OUT • BESIDES • NOW • THEYRE
LIKE • ANY • GOVT • THAT • WANTS • ARMED
MEN • TO • STAY • IN • POWER • SO • THEYLL
NEED • US • EVEN • TO • SURRENDER • ILL •
OFFER • MY • SERVICES • AND • DEMAND • A

POST • SAY • HEAD • OF • POLICE • WE • CAN
QUASH • THIS • SO-CALLED • LAST • WILL
REALLY • HES • NOT • BEEN • HIMSELF • MY
STARS • STILL • SAY • I • MUST • SUCCEED
THE • CHIEF • ALTHOUGH • ITS • HARD • TO

UNDERSTAND • HOW • THAT • CAN • BE • SO •
VERY • PUZZLING • STILL • FLENSBERGS
WHERE • YOUR • CHANCE • MAY • COME • OR •
YOU • CAN • ALWAYS • BITE • INTO • THIS •
ZINC • CAPSULE • & • WHAT • WHAT • WHAT •

DR. JOSEPH GOEBBELS
FORMER MINISTER FOR PROPAGANDA

—1 May 1945.

(Russian troops are within yards of the Bun-
ker. After a brief leavetaking, Goebbels and
Magda climb to the garden to commit sui-
cide.)

Say goodbye to the help, the ranks
Of Stalin-bait. Give too much thanks
To Naumann — Magda's lover: we
Thank him for *all* his loyalty.
Schwaegermann; Rach. After a while
Turn back to them with a sad smile:
We'll save them trouble — no one cares
Just now to carry us upstairs.

Turn away; check your manicure;
Pull on your gloves. Take time; make sure
The hat brim curves though the hat's straight.
Give her your arm. Let the fools wait;
They act like they've someplace to go.
Take the stairs, now. Self-control. Slow.
A slight limp; just enough to see,
Pass on, and infect history.

The rest is silence. Left like sperm
In a stranger's gut, waiting its term,
Each thought, each step lies; the roots spread.
They'll believe in us when we're dead.
When we took "Red Berlin" we found
We always worked best underground.
So; the vile body turns to spirit
That speaks soundlessly. They'll hear it.

CHORUS: OLD LADY BARKEEP

Old Lady Barkeep squealed with laughter
When told she'd be forsaken after
    Her people's sorry loss.
She said, "There's always mobs to swallow
Lies that flatter them and follow
    Some savior to a cross.

"Don't kid yourself — I don't play modest;
As Greed and Cowardice's goddess,
    I thrive on just such ruin.
While humans prowl this globe of yours
I'll never lack for customers.
    By the way, how *you* doin'?"

Acknowledgments

I am indebted, for criticism, information and encouragement, to many colleagues and friends. Donald Hall has gone far beyond generosity with acute intelligence and general abetment. My editor, A. Poulin, Jr., has been a model of insightful suggestion, patience and support. William Patrick provided invaluable counsel. Carl Weber introduced me to Frau Wirtin, and Annette Martin revealed her possibilities. I have had kind assistance from James Merrill, Alice Fulton, John Wood, Gary Miranda, Keith and Rosmarie Waldrop, William Heyen and Lore Segal. Anyone familiar with Henri Coulette's *War of the Secret Agents* will immediately recognize my indebtedness to that work. My wife Kathy, besides her roles as a capacitator, down comforter and tuning fork, has been my first reader and last resort.

I am grateful for periods of residence at Yaddo and the Virginia Center for the Creative Arts. I am also indebted to the Guggenheim Foundation and the University of Delaware Center for Advanced Study for fellowships which released me from teaching duties.

Grateful acknowledgment is made to the editors and publishers of publications in which poems (or earlier versions) first appeared. They are listed below under their original titles:

American Poetry Review: "Adolf Hitler, 1 April 1945," "Adolf Hitler, 20 April 1945," "Eva Braun, 22 April 1945," "Hermann Fegelein, 29 April 1945," "Eva ₿ Hitler, geb. Braun, 30 April 1945" "Adolf Hitler, 30 April 1945," "Reichsmarschall Hermann Goering, 13 April 1945," "Adolf Hitler, 16 April 1945," "Dr. Joseph Goebbels, Minister for Propaganda, 16 April 1945," "Reichsmarschall Hermann Goering, 20 April 1945," "Dr. Joseph Goebbels, 10 April 1945" and "Dr. Joseph Goebbels, Minister for Propaganda, 23 April 1945"; *Georgia Review:* "Albert Speer, 18 April 1945" and "Albert Speer, 20 April 1945"; *Kentucky Poetry Review:* "Dr. Joseph Goebbels, 1 April 1945"; *Kenyon Review:* "Double Chorus, 1 April 1945", "Heinrich Himmler, Reichs-fuehrer SS, 20 April 1945," "Magda Goebbels, 30 April 1945" and "Heinrich Himmler, Former Reichsfuehrer SS, 1 May 1945"; *Michigan Quarterly Review:* "Reichsmarschall Hermann Goering, 16 April 1945," "Eva Braun, 10 April, 1945,' and "Helga Goebbels, 29 April 1945"; *New Virginia Review:* "Heinrich Himmler" (cast of characters for *The Fuehrer Bunker*); *The Noiseless Spider:* "Dr. Joseph Goebbels, 27 April 1945"; *Princeton University Library Chronicle:* "Traudl Junge, 1 May 1945"; *Salmagundi:* "The Goebbels Children," "Magda Goebbels, 1 May 1945" and "Reichsmarschall Hermann Goering, 22 April 1945"; *Scarab:* "Lt. Gen. Helmuth 'Crusher Karl' Weidling, Commander 56th Panzer Corps, 23 April 1945"; *Seneca Review:* "Dr. Joseph Goebbels, 19 April 1945," "Magda Goebbels, 19 April 1945," "Dr. Joseph Goebbels, 22 April 1945," "Magda Goebbels, 22

About the Author

Responsible for the emergence of American confessional poetry, W. D. Snodgrass won the 1960 Pulitzer Prize for Poetry with his first book, *Heart's Needle.* He saw much of our domestic suffering as occurring against a backdrop of a more universal suffering inherent in the whole of human experience. Snodgrass followed that astonishing work with *After Experience* and, later, *The Führer Bunker: A Cycle of Poems in Progress,* published by BOA Editions in 1977. The book was nominated for the National Book Critics Circle Award for Poetry and produced by Wynn Handman for The American Place Theatre.

Born in Wilkinsburg, Pennsylvania, and educated at Geneva College and the University of Iowa, Snodgrass has taught at Cornell, the University of Rochester, Wayne State University, Syracuse University, Old Dominion University, and the University of Delaware. He has received fellowships from the Guggenheim and Ingram Merrill Foundations, the Academy of American Poets, the National Institute of Arts and Letters and the National Endowment for the Arts.

BOA EDITIONS, LTD.
AMERICAN POETS CONTINUUM SERIES